J
B
JACKSON Devaney, John

Bo Jackson

BO JACKSON

A STAR FOR ALL SEASONS

BO JACKSON

A STAR FOR ALL SEASONS

by John Devaney

Walker and Company

New York

First published in the United States of America in 1988
by the Walker Publishing Company, Inc.

Published simultaneously in Canada by Thomas Allen & Son
Canada, Limited, Markham, Ontario.

LIBRARY OF CONGRESS
Library of Congress Cataloging-in-Publication Data

Devaney, John.
    Bo Jackson : a star for all seasons / by John Devaney.
        p.   cm.
    Includes index.
    Summary: A biography of the first major league to play in both pro baseball
and football.
        ISBN 0-8027-6818-0. ISBN 0-8027-6819-9 (lib. bdg.)
        1. Jackson, Bo—Juvenile literature. 2. Baseball players—United
States—Biography—Juvenile literature. 3. Football players—United
States—Biography—Juvenile literature. [1. Jackson, Bo.
2. Baseball players. 3. Football players. 4. Afro-Americans—
Biography.] I. Title.
GV865.J28D48   1988
796.332'092'4—dc19
[B]
[92]   88-17233
                                                          CIP
                                                           AC

Printed in the United States of America

10   9   8   7   6   5   4   3   2   1

For Danny Thomas

ACKNOWLEDGEMENTS

A number of people were most helpful to me in gathering material and photos for this book. I thank in particular the people at Auburn's Sports Information Department, and those with the Kansas City Royals and Los Angeles Raiders. My thanks also to Bill Harris, the Downtown Athletic Club and its always helpful Marge Koenig for photos of Heisman Trophy winners. And special thanks to Amy Shields and George Sullivan.

CONTENTS

BO JACKSON

A STAR FOR ALL SEASONS

BOAR

Boar led his gang of twenty teenage boys up the steep hill. The boys called this hill The Mountain. Looking behind them, Boar's gang could see the streets of Bessemer. Black smoke curled from the smokestacks of the Alabama city's steel mills.

Boar's gang prowled for trouble like wild dogs. They broke windows. They stole bikes. They threw stones at other gangs. They bashed heads with baseball bats.

The thirteen-year-old Boar scared even eighteen-year olds. "Boar will hit you in the head with a rock," one boy told his older brother. "No one throws a rock harder than Boar. Boar hits me in the head two or three times a week. Look at my head. It's always got bumps on it."

Boar laughed when teachers called him a bully. He liked being a bully. "I do my share of being bad," he told people. The fun of hurting people showed in the way his small, deep-set eyes glinted as he spoke of being a terror.

A boy saw a rock dance in Boar's hand. He cowered behind a boulder and shouted, "Don't hit me, Boar, don't hit me!"

Boar laughed. He walked up a trail to a rise. "Look there!" he shouted, pointing downward.

The boys ran to the rise. They saw a pen filled with dozens of grunting pigs.

Boar's long right arm flashed backward. The rock whizzed through the air. It thudded between the eyes of a pig.

The pig keeled over, shrieking. Blood gushed. Other pigs squealed in terror.

Boar grabbed another rock and threw. His gang grabbed for rocks.

A door slammed at a nearby house. "Someone's coming!" a boy shouted.

Boar and his gang ran down the hill, dust billowing behind them. Boar laughed loudly. He'd be back to get more pigs. He'd done a lot of hurting. Now maybe it was time to do some killing.

That night Boar lay in his bed and thought about killing pigs. Boar lived in a small three-room house in Bessemer, a suburb of Birmingham, Alabama. His nine brothers and sisters were squeezed into the house with their mother. A single parent, she worked twelve to sixteen hours a day as a cleaning woman at a nearby motel.

She tried to raise her children to believe in God, go to church on Sundays, and read the Bible. "We don't have much," she often said, "but we do have love for God and for each other."

Except for Boar. He seemed to want only to hurt. "You'll end up in the penitentiary before you're twenty-one," she told Boar. He grinned.

Several days later Boar and his gang marched up The Mountain. As the gang came closer the pigs stared, their small eyes showing their fright. The boys gripped rocks and bats. They rushed into the pen. They swung the bats and flung the rocks.

Pigs cried with pain. Blood spurted from broken heads and torn hides. Boar roared with laughter as he swung a bat at a dying pig. Bodies of dead pigs were strewn across the pen.

A gun's roar stopped bats in midair. Boar saw a man holding a smoking gun. The man saw Boar. Boar knew what the man was thinking: "It's that Jackson kid making trouble again."

The boys dashed down the hill. Boar, the swiftest, led the pack. No one turned, fearing another roar of the gun.

Boar rushed to his house. He ripped off his bloodied pants. He was slipping on fresh pants when he heard a car screech to a stop outside his house. He looked out the window and saw the man who had fired the gun. The man knocked at the door.

The face of Boar's mother hardened like stone. The man was telling her that Boar and his gang had killed three thousand dollars' worth of pigs.

Boar's mother glared at Boar. She turned back to the man and said, "If you want to make arrangements to send him to reform school, I'm all for it. I've been telling him all along that one day he'd be sent to prison."

Eight years later, on a spring day in 1984, the state of Alabama's number one sports hero stood in front of a classroom filled with blind and deaf children. Their faces glowed. This hero ran for touchdowns on the Auburn University football team. He hit soaring home runs for Auburn's baseball team. He ran so fast for Auburn's track team that soon he would be trying out for America's 1984 Olympic team.

The sports hero liked to speak to kids. He stuttered when he spoke to grown-ups. But he spoke smoothly to kids. They made him feel relaxed.

The blind and deaf children attended the Helen Keller School in Talladega, Alabama. They had written to the hero and asked him to come to speak at their sports dinner.

Few of the kids had expected the hero to say yes. He had said no when baseball's New York Yankees offered him a quarter of a million dollars to play for them. He had said no when a pro football team offered him half a million dollars to join them. Baseball scouts said he could be another Mickey Mantle. Football scouts said he could be

3

another O. J. Simpson. One day, scouts said, he would be in both baseball's and football's Halls of Fame.

Scouts, reporters, and radio and TV interviewers clamored to talk to the hero. Nearly always he said no. But the hero had said yes to the children in Talladega.

The blind children kept their eyes on where his voice came from. The deaf children watched the moving fingers of a woman who changed the hero's words into sign language.

"I'd like to share my past with you," the hero said. "In third grade I was so bad I'd bully the sixth graders." He told of broken windows and stolen bikes.

"In my life there have been three roads. There has been a high road, a low road, and—in between—a just road. Right now I'm on that just road. With God's help, I'm about to get to the top, to the high road."

And then he told the children how Boar Jackson, bully, became Bo Jackson, hero.

But first he had to tell them about Vincent.

VINCENT

"Go ahead! Hit me! I dare you!"

Eight-year-old Vincent Jackson pulled up his shirt and bared his belly. "Hit me right here!" he shouted to his fourteen-year-old cousin. "You can't hurt me!"

The fourteen-year-old cousin frowned. He knew a punch to the belly could kill a small boy. But Vincent dared him.

"Okay," the cousin said. He drew back his fist and rammed it into Vincent's belly.

Vincent laughed. "I got the strongest stomach you ever saw," he said. "No one can hurt me."

"You are as tough as a wild boar," his cousin said with awe in his voice.

A boar is a wild pig that terrorizes other animals. "He sure scares me," his brothers and sisters said of Vincent. They began to call him Boar.

Boar's mother had named him Vincent. Her favorite actor was Vincent Edwards, who played Dr. Ben Casey on a TV show. Vincent was born in Bessemer, Alabama, on November 30, 1962. Vincent's mother and father were separated. But Vincent often saw his father, a husky steelworker named A. D. Adams, who lived in Bessemer.

Vincent's mother's name had been Jackson. Her parents, Vincent's grandfather and grandmother, lived a few houses away. Mr. and Mrs. Jackson often took care of Vincent.

Vincent was the eighth of his mother's ten children. The ten grew up in a three-room house. There was a kitchen, which his mother used as a bedroom. There was a living room, which had a gas heater, and another bedroom. "We slept," Vincent once said, "wherever we could find a vacant spot in the house. Most of the time I would get right down in front of the little gas heater in the living room. Some nights I didn't have a cover to put over me. But I knew that my mom would take care of me."

There are poor people and there are, as Abraham Lincoln once said, "dirt-poor people." Vincent Jackson grew up dirt poor. "We didn't have anything," he often said. "I realized early on that I was starting at the bottom."

Vincent's older brothers and sisters pushed and shoved him. Vincent couldn't push and shove back. But, playing in the street, he learned how to push, shove, and bully other children.

Once a girl tried to snatch a Ping-Pong paddle out of his hands. Boar picked up a baseball bat and hit her across the head.

Vincent attended the Raimond Elementary School. As a third grader he asked the track coach, "Can I run on the team?"

"No, only fourth to sixth graders are allowed on the team."

The next day Vincent wiggled into a line of runners at the start of a sixty-yard dash. At the gun, Vincent sprinted out in front. He finished far ahead of even the sixth graders.

The coach looked at Vincent. "You are now on the track team," the coach said.

"I've been running and jumping and throwing since I can remember," Vincent once said. "Being good at sports always came easy to me."

But being a bully also came easy to Vincent "Boar" Jackson.

"Boy, you give me that dollar you got there in your hand." Boar was speaking to another fourth grader.

"That's my lunch money."

"Give it to me or I'll bounce rocks off your head for a week."

The boy gave Boar the dollar. "Now I have no money to buy my lunch," the boy said.

"Here's fifty cents. You can buy milk and cookies."

"Thanks."

"But you got to pay me back one dollar by tomorrow," Boar said, grinning.

"Why?"

"I just loaned you fifty cents, didn't I? And I charge you fifty cents on the loan. Fifty plus fifty makes one dollar."

"But you just took my dollar," the boy said, beginning to cry.

"What dollar are you talking about? And if you don't pay me back my dollar by tomorrow, I'll bounce two rocks off your head."

As a fifth grader, Boar scared even eighth graders into giving him their lunch money. He hired other boys to beat up bigger boys and take their money.

His gang ran the streets. They threw stones through shop windows. They stole bikes of other kids.

Parents and shopkeepers begged Boar's mother to stop his bullying. She had to work half the day at the motel, where she cleaned rooms. She couldn't lock Boar in the house. But she warned him that the police would put him in jail if he kept on being a hoodlum.

His mother made him join the neighborhood Little League team. When a coach put a baseball in his hand, Boar looked at it, surprised. The ball felt so light—not nearly as heavy as those rocks he'd been throwing for as long as he could remember.

Boar threw what looked like a white streak past frightened Little League hitters. Coaches feared he would injure a batter. "No more Little League for you," they told

Boar. Soon, only eleven years old, he threw fastballs past fifteen-year-olds in Pony League games.

"But I hate pitching," he told a friend. "There's no action on the mound. You just stand there and throw the ball."

Coaches let him play shortstop and centerfield, his two favorite positions. As a shortstop he threw out runners with line-drive throws. First basemen winced as they caught the ball. And in centerfield Boar raced left, right, long, and short to spear line drives.

His speed astonished other players. Once he hit a ground ball that bounced on one hop right back to the pitcher. The pitcher turned, threw to first—and saw Boar flash across the bag ahead of the throw.

By the summer of 1974, the eleven-year-old Boar stood tall and lean. His bony shoulders and sinewy arms and legs felt as hard as steel pipes.

His mother often said that Vincent was like none of her other children. She noticed that he stammered and stuttered when he talked to other grown-ups. Yet he didn't stammer when he spoke to her. "I know he's a terror," she told neighbors. "But I get the feeling that Vincent is going to grow up to be somebody."

One day she came home from grocery shopping. Boar helped her carry in the bags. "You know," he told his mother, "I want to go to college."

None of her other children had gone to college. "I don't know how you're going to go because I don't have the money to send you," his mother said.

Boar said nothing. He knew his father and mother didn't have the money to send him to college. But a dream began to form in his mind—Boar attending college, Boar receiving a diploma.

His mother told him he was more likely to go to prison than college. Once she caught him stealing money she had put aside to pay for her insurance. "Thieves wind up doing time," she warned him for the hundredth time. Boar only grinned.

Some of his gang smoked marijuana. One day Boar found a plastic bag with a marijuana cigarette inside. That evening, alone in the bathroom, he smoked the cigarette.

He felt strange. He didn't like what was happening to his head.

Dazed, he wandered into the kitchen. He threw open the refrigerator door and gobbled down food. Then waves of sickness rocked his head. This was what his friends meant when they said, "Let's get high."

Boar wanted no more of it. Still shaky and sick the next day, he promised himself that never again would he touch a drug.

He was still Boar the bully. But one day he picked on the wrong boy—and the boy, a husky ninth grader, knocked Boar out with a punch.

Boar went home and found an old .22-caliber hunting rifle and waited by the side of a road. He saw the ninth grader coming toward him. The boy's figure came closer in the gun's sight. Boar's finger curled around the trigger.

He'd go to reform school if he was caught. One of Boar's older brothers had gone to reform school. He had told Boar what prison was like—the clang of metal doors behind you, the cries in the night, the fear of being hurt.

Boar knew he could never live cooped up. He put down the gun and carried it home.

Boar always had to be doing something—bullying, playing baseball, racing around a track. He dreaded the summers when kids hung around a Bessemer recreation hall, too hot to play basketball or baseball. It was in the summer of 1976, when Boar was thirteen, that he and his gang left the recreation hall to climb The Mountain. There they found a pen full of pigs and three thousand dollars' worth of trouble.

Boar stared at the man who had fired the gun. His mother had just told the man he could take Boar away to the reform school—the dreaded reform school that had terrified Boar's brother.

Boar hardly heard the words as the man said to him, "Boar, would you be willing to try to save yourself from jail?"

BO ⚾

Boar looked at the man. What did he mean?

The man said he would talk to the person who owned the pigs. Maybe, just maybe, if Boar and his friends paid the man the three thousand dollars that the dead pigs had cost, the owner wouldn't call the police.

Boar thanked the man for trying to help him. And a few days later, Boar and his gang began to wash cars, run errands, mow lawns—whatever odd jobs they could find. For the next six months they worked mornings and nights, before and after school. By early in 1977, the boys had paid back, bit by bit, the three thousand dollars.

Boar had done some thinking during that time. He knew how close he had come to the horrors of prison. He would never come that close again, he told himself. Instead, he decided, he would find a way to do what he had told his mother he wanted to do—go to college.

Maybe he could work his way through college. He had enjoyed making money to pay for the pigs. Somehow, he told himself, he would find a way to go to college and be the first in his family to win a degree.

Boar had been too busy pushing, shoving, and bullying his way through school to study. He was a year or two older than most of the boys in his class when he graduated from elementary school. In the fall of 1978, three months shy of his sixteenth birthday, he entered McAdory High School in McCalla, another suburb of Birmingham.

He made friends at McAdory. He decided they would be his new friends. Most of his old gang, he realized, would end up standing on street corners in Birmingham with their brains numbed by alcohol and drugs. Some would go from those street corners to prison.

His new friends knew nothing about the wild Boar in his past. When Boar told them his nickname, they shortened it to Bo.

"Hey, Bo, you got to try out for the football team."

"I don't like football," Bo said. "My favorite sport is track, then baseball. And my mom said she doesn't want me coming home all sore and limping."

But to please his new friends, Bo decided to try out for the football team.

They sat in the stands, shouting "Go, Bo!" as Bo, dressed in his first football uniform, trotted onto the field for a scrimmage against McAdory's B team. Varsity football coach Dick Atchison, a solidly built man, stood on the sideline watching the ninth graders trying out for the B team.

The lanky Bo—he stood about five feet ten but weighed only 150 pounds—crouched on the defensive line. A ball carrier raced for the sideline. Bo sped after him, caught him from behind, and threw him for a loss.

Coach Atchison looked at his list of ninth graders. "That Vincent Jackson has blazing speed," he said to an assistant. "If he gets a little heavier, we can use him next season on defense with the varsity."

The coach talked to Bo and learned to his surprise that Bo had never played a football game in his life. Coach Atchison told Bo to try out for the track team that following spring. "For your age," he told Bo, "you're very fast."

One day Bo came home limping after a bruising practice with the B team. His mother shouted at him, "I told you not to play football." But she calmed down when

Bo explained that the season would soon end. "And if I'm good enough," Bo told his mother, "maybe I could get one of those football scholarships and go to college free."

Bo got passing grades at McAdory. "I have to," he told his mother, "or the coach won't let me try out for the track team. And track is still my favorite sport."

In the spring of 1979, Bo tried out for the track team. "I have seniors who are faster than you," Atchison told Bo, "but you're terrific in the hurdles, the high jump, the triple, and the long jump. Practice those events."

That summer, his freshman year over, Bo steered clear of his old gang hanging out on Bessemer street corners. He walked out into the country where he could enjoy another sport—fishing. "This is the place I'd rather go than anywhere else," he told a cousin one day as they sat on the bank of a small pond, their fishing poles in hand. "You can't hear a thing. No cars, nobody. I just come here to relax. If I catch a fish, I'll throw it back."

Coach Atchison whistled softly when he saw Bo walk into the football locker room in the fall of 1979. Bo, almost seventeen, stood close to six feet tall, towering over the other players. But what startled the coach was how Bo had filled out across the chest and shoulders. Bo weighed about 170 pounds—"and all of it," said an awed teammate, "is as hard as concrete."

The coach asked Bo, "Have you been lifting weights?" Muscles bulged on Bo's long arms. He looked like a wrestler.

Bo never lifted weights. Exercising bored him. He always had to be on the move. "I just eat my favorite food—liver," he said.

How did he get so strong? "God's blessing," Bo said simply. Like his mother, Bo had become deeply religious. "God gave me strength and speed," he said. "It's up to me to make the best use of those blessings."

His old street-gang pals often stopped Bo when they saw him walking home after school. Once they pushed a bottle of liquor into his hands and said, "Let's have fun like the old days."

Bo handed back the bottle. He knew that Coach Atchison would bounce him off the team if he heard he'd been drinking.

"Coach Atchison," Bo later said, "is the man who really got me off the streets, off the bad road. It was him and sports that made me want to make something of myself."

Bo won a starter's position on Coach Atchison's team, which was one of the state's best football teams. A defensive end, he rammed over blockers like a battering ram and knocked down ball carriers. Near the end of the season, Coach Atchison told Bo: "You're getting bigger and faster. I am going to play you both ways. You'll still play end on defense. But now I want you to carry the ball for us on offense."

Carrying the ball, Bo ripped through tacklers' arms as though they were butter. He shot away from pursuers with his sprinter's speed. He gained 400 yards in the 1979 season, more than half the yardage gained by other McAdory runners during the entire season.

In the spring of 1980, Bo scooted back to the track team. He competed in all ten events of the decathlon. The decathlon is track's most grueling event. An athlete must compete in ten events, from the 60-yard dash to the mile run. He must fling a discus and put the shot. He must leap in events like the high jump and pole vault. A person who wins the Olympic decathlon is often called "the world's greatest athlete."

At the state of Alabama track championships that spring of 1980, Bo, only a sophomore, competed against juniors and seniors. He finished first in several of the decathlon's races and finished in third place in the overall scoring for the decathlon title. His third-place finish helped McAdory win the state championship.

McAdory's stocky baseball coach, Terry Brasseale, talked to Bo, who told the coach how he had loved

14

baseball in the Pony League. Bo said he liked baseball better than football. He played football only because his high school pals had begged him to try out for the team.

"Track is my first love," Bo told the baseball coach, "but if I couldn't go to college as a football player, I would love to be like my baseball idol, Reggie Jackson, and play in the big leagues." Bo had watched the 1977 World Series with glowing eyes as Reggie Jackson slugged five home runs for the New York Yankees in that Series. As a little boy, Bo had thought he wanted to hit home runs like Hank Aaron, another idol. But now he dreamed of hitting home runs like Reggie Jackson.

Coach Brasseale asked Bo to play on the McAdory baseball team. "I'll share you with the track team," the coach said.

The two coaches scheduled track meets and baseball games so that Bo could compete in both sports. Often, Bo raced through ten events at a track meet, sped over to the baseball field, jerked on a uniform, and ran out onto the diamond.

From the mound he zipped baseballs at batters. "It looks like a white pea shooting at you," one hitter said of Bo's fastball. But Bo still did not like to pitch. What he liked was to roam the outfield snaring long drives. What he loved was hitting. Teammates stared with awe in their eyes as the husky sophomore drove line drives over distant fences.

When the 1980 football season began, Bo stood six feet tall and weighed 185 pounds. Now a junior, Bo blocked for the football team's number one ball carrier, who was a senior. In one game, Bo knocked aside one tackler, threw a flying block on a second, then jumped to his feet and shot ahead of the McAdory ball carrier, blasting aside a third defender. The McAdory runner cantered into the end zone.

Bo was the team's number two ball carrier. He carried the ball for 800 yards in the 1980 season, almost as many yards as the number one runner. He played every minute of every game, shifting to play defense when the other team got the ball. As a defensive end, he crashed through blockers to upend passers and mow down runners.

Then, when track started in the spring, Bo won the state decathlon championship. He hurried to baseball games after track meets. He pitched no-hitters. He stole bases—90 in 91 attempts. He smashed home runs. He got a hit almost once every two at-bats, batting .450.

One day, Coach Brasseale pointed to a tall man wearing a baseball cap. He said to Bo, "See that man over there?"

"Yes. Who is he?"

"He's a scout for the New York Yankees. He lives in Birmingham. He heard about your hitting and pitching. The Yankees want him to scout you."

Unknown to Bo, Yankee officials back in New York had put his name high on the list of high school players they wanted to sign.

By the fall of 1981, Bo's senior year, he stood six feet one and weighed 205 pounds. "He has a body as hard as a sculpted Greek statue," one McAdory gym teacher said.

Bo was now the football team's number one runner. He gained 1,400 yards in the fall of 1981, even though Coach Atchison let him carry the ball only eleven or twelve times a game. The coach didn't want Bo to score so many touchdowns that the other team would be embarrassed.

On defense he seemed to be all over the field. In one game he knocked down a passer, but just before the passer fell, he lofted the ball to a receiver.

Bo jumped to his feet. He took off after the receiver, who had caught the ball ten yards away from Bo. Bo caught him from behind and tackled him.

Bo never left the field during all of McAdory's games that senior year. He ran back the ball when the opposing team punted or kicked off to McAdory. He punted. He kicked field goals. In Bo's three seasons on the varsity team, during which he played almost every minute of every game—"He's never hurt," Coach Atchison said—

McAdory won twenty-seven of thirty-one games.

College football coaches phoned him every day from as far as California. Bo now knew his dream would come true—he would go to college.

In the spring of 1982 he still shuttled between track meets and baseball games. He won the state decathlon championship for the second year in a row. He set a state record—9.54 seconds—for the 100-yard dash. In baseball he slugged 20 home runs, tying the record for the most home runs ever hit in one season by any U.S. high school baseball player. He batted .447, still getting a hit almost every two times at bat.

Each year a McAdory school official picked the school's outstanding athlete. Everyone knew he would win.

But the official said there would be no athlete picked in 1982.

Black and white students shouted their anger. Bo had set school, state, and national records in track, baseball, and football. "The school has to pick Bo," black students argued. But some white students said the official probably knew something and so maybe Bo didn't deserve the honor.

Fearing fist-fights between students, McAdory school officials called a meeting. Hundreds of students jammed into the school library. Insults shot back and forth. Fists clenched. Mouths twisted in anger.

The library door suddenly swung open. Heads turned. The students saw Bo.

"Listen, all of you," Bo said, his husky voice cutting through the hush. "I didn't come to McAdory to win a popularity contest. I came for an education. Now enough of this junk and back to classes."

Boys and girls stared. One girl began to cry.

Dick Atchison sat in the room. "It was incredible when he came in and said that," the coach said years later as he told how Bo was finally given the award. "It stunned everybody. It showed that Bo Jackson was more than a football player."

QUITTER

"How much—a quarter of a million dollars?"

Bo's mother stumbled over the words. She shook her head in wonder. A quarter of a million dollars to play baseball?

That New York Yankees' scout, the one in the cap who had been watching Bo since his junior year, had raved to Yankee officials about Bo. The officials were impressed. Each year the big league teams select the best high school and college players in the annual baseball draft. Of the hundreds of players selected, Bo had been picked second—by the Yankees. To lure Bo into playing for them (after playing first for a Yankee minor league team), the Yankees were offering Bo a quarter of a million dollars.

His mother talked to Bo about all that money—more than the Jackson family had ever expected any one of them could earn in a lifetime. His mother told Bo she hoped he would turn down the quarter of a million dollars.

"If you want to play baseball," his mother said, "you do what you want. But you know that I want you to be the first of my children to graduate from college."

Bo told the scout he had to say "no" to the $250,000. Bo wanted to go to college on a football scholarship. He couldn't play college football if he signed a pro baseball contract.

The scout stared, amazed that Bo, raised in poverty, would say no to a quarter of a million dollars. The next day he met Bo near McAdory. He thrust a paper at Bo. "Just sign this," the scout said, "and I'll give you this." He showed Bo a check for a quarter of a million dollars.

"No," Bo said, he was going to college.

"You and Bo must be crazy," a neighbor told Bo's mother.

"I raised ten kids without any money," Bo's mother said. "Why do I need any now?"

"And what about Bo?" the woman asked.

"He just values being happy more than being rich," his mother said.

"I would probably spend four years in the minor leagues," Bo explained to friends. "In that time I could play football in college, run track, play baseball, and get a college degree that can help me later on. I am getting four things by going to college—baseball, track, football, and an education. If I sign with the Yankees, I get only one—baseball."

College football coaches begged him to come to their campuses. Bo said he wanted to stay in Alabama. That meant two choices for most Alabama athletes—the University of Alabama or Auburn University in the little town of Auburn. Some Alabama students sneered at Auburn, calling it a "cowpatch college."

Alabama ranked almost every year among the nation's top ten teams. Bo idolized the Crimson Tide's coach, Bear Bryant. Watching the Crimson Tide on TV, Bo yelled—as did all 'Bama fans—"Ro*lllll*, Tide, Ro*lllll* . . ."

A 'Bama coach talked to Bo. He told Bo that 'Bama got all the state's best athletes. Auburn, he said, got the leftovers. Alabama had so many great players, the coach said, that Bo would have to wait his turn to be a starter—probably until his junior year.

Bo said he didn't like sitting on a bench and wasting two years. He said he was going to talk to Auburn head coach Pat Dye.

Auburn had become a doormat that other teams wiped their feet on. The season before, Auburn's Tigers—"pussycats," some fans called them—lost more games than they won. Auburn had not beaten Alabama in their annual battle in ten years.

"You go to Auburn," the Alabama coach said, "and you'll be on a losing team for four straight years."

Auburn's new coach, the towering Pat Dye, told Bo how Auburn's team was growing stronger. Coach Dye was bringing in more than twenty high school stars for the fall of 1982. He told Bo that Bo could compete in track and baseball each spring and skip spring football practice.

Bo made up his mind.

Big grins spread across the faces of the Auburn varsity players. "Send in more of those hotshot freshmen," one 260-pound tackle growled.

Under bright lights at Auburn's huge Jordan-Haire Stadium, the 1982 Auburn team scrimmaged to get ready for its opening game against Wake Forest. Coach Dye sent in his high school stars to run against the varsity. The burly varsity players bounced the freshmen back onto the seats of their pants.

"I ran over guys in high school," one battered freshman running back said. "But those guys are bigger and faster than anything I ever saw in high school."

Bo ran out onto the field. He wore the number 34. That number was also worn by college football's most famous player, Herschel Walker, a speedy and huge running back at the University of Georgia. In two years Herschel Walker, by now a junior, had dashed for so many touchdowns that Georgia, once an ordinary team, had become a national power.

The varsity players stared at Bo—another hotshot freshman to bounce up into the air.

The quarterback called signals. He took the snap. He spun and pitched the ball to Bo.

Two linebackers converged on Bo. Bo faked left, then

A starter as a running back after his first game for Auburn, Bo gained 4,303 yards and scored 43 touchdowns in four seasons. Coach Pat Dye once said he thought Bo a better athlete than Walter Payton or O. J. Simpson—Hall of Fame stature–running backs.

Photo courtesy of Auburn University.

roared right—and the linebackers' hands grasped air. Sprawled on the grass, they stared at Bo's flying heels.

Bo sped past the 50-yard line. A safety shot forward to meet him. Bo lowered his helmet and rammed into the safety, who flew backward. Bo trampled right over his chest.

Bo galloped for touchdown after touchdown against the varsity. The players stared at him.

"Everybody," said one coach, "knew this guy was something different."

After the scrimmage, Coach Dye took Bo aside. "I think you can be our Herschel Walker, Bo," the coach said. "Would you like to do that?"

"Yes," Bo said. Later that week Bo set himself three goals to accomplish during the next four years—to gain more yards than any Auburn back in history, to win the Heisman Trophy awarded to college football's number one player, and to be the first player picked by the pros in the 1986 National Football League draft.

The roaring of sixty thousand fans filled Jordan-Haire Stadium. In this first game of the 1982 season, Auburn had just pushed through the Wake Forest line for a touchdown. The Tigers led Wake Forest, 7–0.

Bo stood on the sideline watching as his roommate, Lionel "Little Train" James, came off the field. "Way to go!" Bo shouted, applauding the offense for scoring the season's first touchdown.

Bo glanced at Coach Dye. He wondered, Will coach let me play in this opening game?

Minutes later Wake Forest punted the ball to Auburn. "Offense!" a coach shouted.

The offensive players strapped on helmets to run into the game. Coach Dye turned and shouted, "Go in, Bo!"

The crowd erupted. News of Bo's streaks through the varsity had spread across the campus. Everyone wanted to know if this Bo Jackson was another Herschel Walker.

The chunky Little Train ran with Bo to the huddle. "When we pitch you the ball," Little Train said, grinning, "take off."

Wake Forest linemen stared at the six-feet-two, 222-pound Bo. They had heard all about him. Bo knew he was a marked man.

In the huddle the Auburn quarterback called for a pitch to Bo.

The quarterback, taking the snap, flipped the ball to Bo. He sprinted for the sideline, faked going left, and then weaved through two off-balance tacklers. He spun forward.

22

Two tacklers spilled him after a gain of 11 yards for an Auburn first down. Bo ran back to the huddle, hearing a chant he would hear for the next four years—"Go, Bo, Go . . . Go, Bo . . ."

Auburn drove to the Wake Forest 1-yard line, and Bo dived over the middle of the Wake Forest line for his first Tiger touchdown.

Auburn led, 21–10, as the fourth period began. Auburn pushed the ball to the Wake Forest 43-yard line. Auburn's quarterback called another pitchout of the ball to Bo.

On the snap Bo raced toward the sideline. He turned and saw the ball spin toward him. A tackler angled toward him. Bo flew by him. At the sideline he swerved to curl downfield, three tacklers chasing at his heels.

Then Bo showed them—and the crowd—his world-class sprinter's speed. Like a jet plane being chased by a lumbering seaplane, Bo flew away from the tacklers. He raced down the sideline and trotted into the end zone with his second touchdown of the day.

The next day's newspapers called the game "The Bo Show." Auburn had won, 28–10, and Bo led all the runners with 123 yards in only 10 carries, an astonishing average of 12 yards a try. Those 123 yards were the most ever gained in one game by an Auburn freshman. Bo had won a starter's job—a prize only injury would take from him over the next four years.

Bo had come to hate practice during the week. He dreaded the endless situps and pushups, the lung-searing wind sprints across the field. Whenever he stopped, an assistant coach shouted angrily at him.

"I'll do my running in the game," Bo said.

"You'll run now," an assistant growled, "or you'll ride the bench in the game."

Frowning, Bo ran. But he disliked being threatened with punishment like a schoolboy.

The next week Bo ran for 99 yards in 13 tries. He ran

back kickoffs another 59 yards. Auburn squeezed out a 21–19 victory. "Bo," said Coach Dye, "was the key to our win."

Assistant coaches nagged Bo all during the week. Once, when Bo stopped to catch his breath during a run, a coach yanked his arm. "Don't you ever do that to me again if you value your life," Bo snapped.

That night he told Little Train: "Those assistants treat us like little boys. I am a grown man. I see those coaches slapping players across the head. I go out to practice, not to get slapped around."

Auburn had roared off to its best start in ten years, winning five of its first six games. Bo led the Auburn runners with 461 yards, second in the Southeastern Conference only to Herschel Walker's 750. Herschel had gained an average of 5 yards a run, while Bo's average topped that—7 yards a run.

Auburn lost to Florida, 19–17. Coach Dye ranted that most of the Tigers, Bo included, had stumbled through the game, playing listlessly.

That week the assistant coaches whiplashed the players with angry words. Bo had to run dozens of exhausting wind sprints. When players slowed down, coaches meted out a dreaded punishment—five or ten "stadiums," which meant running up all the steps of the Jordan-Haire Stadium from bottom to top. Five or ten stadiums could leave a player too leg-weary to walk for an hour.

"Bo is back in form," Coach Dye said excitedly, watching Bo run wind sprints. But later Bo said angrily to a player, "I wish those coaches would let me get ready in my own way."

Georgia—and Herschel Walker—came to Jordan-Haire the next Saturday. Newspapers called the game the Bo Jackson–Herschel Walker duel. One reporter wrote: "Auburn has to stop Herschel, Georgia has to stop Bo."

Georgia stopped Bo. Each time he got the ball, at least two huge Georgia Bulldogs waited to pounce on him. He gained only 58 yards. But Auburn could not stop Herschel.

He gained 177 yards. He scored 2 touchdowns. Georgia won, 19–13.

Bo sat glumly in the dressing room. Anger boiled inside him—anger that he had gained so few yards. The coaches would drive him harder and more brutally during the week. Why should he take it? And who needed all these demands from fans, sportswriters, players, and coaches—gain more yards . . . gain more yards . . . gain more yards . . .

I want out, he told himself. *I want out!*

Two days later he packed his clothes. He borrowed a car and drove to the Auburn bus station. He walked up to the ticket window to order a ticket back to Bessemer.

It was time to go home. Time to leave college. Time to forget that college degree. It was time to quit.

VICTORY

A porter swept a brush across the floor of the bus station. Four people stood in line waiting for the last bus. Bo sat on a bench in a shadowy corner.

"We're closing after this bus," the porter told Bo. Bo glanced up at a clock—the time was almost one o'clock in the morning.

Bo had been sitting here for almost five hours. Two questions shouted at each other across his mind. Should he quit college and go home? Or should he take more of the brutal practices that he hated?

What would people back in Bessemer say if he came home? He could guess. Just another kid who could have been a sports star but who didn't stick it out—and ended up hanging out on street corners. Or going to jail. Or dying of an overdose.

Bo stood up. He walked slowly to a phone booth. He called an assistant coach. He confessed he was out of his room. All players were supposed to be in their rooms by midnight.

The coach told Bo to go back to his dormitory room. The next day Coach Dye talked to Bo. For being out after midnight, Bo had to run a hundred "stadiums"—a hundred trips up and down the hundreds of stadium steps.

Bo ran the hundred stadiums. Coach Dye called him into his office.

"Bo," the husky coach said, "your being on the football team gives Auburn people hope that one day the Tigers will topple Alabama and stand tall as the state's number one team."

Bo nodded. He knew he'd been wrong. But he still hated practice.

Coach Dye worried. Bo might go home. And Bo, he now knew, could be his Herschel Walker.

Coach Dye told the other coaches to go easier on Bo. "He knows his body," Coach Dye said. "He knows how to get it ready for a game."

Bo no longer had to lift weights. He stopped doing situps while other players grunted and sweated through dozens. Players grumbled. "Bo is the coach's pet," they muttered to one another.

The Iron Bowl. That is the name given to the annual battle between Alabama and Auburn. The entire state seems to stop in its tracks to watch this struggle. When Auburn beats Alabama, Tiger fans roll streams of paper down the streets of Auburn. The paper rises as high as car tires and stretches for blocks. In Tuscaloosa, when 'Bama wins, car horns blare all night.

'Bama Coach Bear Bryant once said that his Tide liked to beat the nation's top teams like Notre Dame. "But nothing is more important," he added, "than beating that team from the cow college on the other side of the state."

Some seventy-six thousand fans filled Legion Field in Birmingham for the 1982 battle. As usual, it was the last game of the season for both teams. Alabama fans roared, "Rollll . . . Tide . . . Rollll . . ." Auburn fans screamed, "Warrrr . . . Eagle . . . Warrrr . . ." From kickoff to final gun, the noise of cheers and chants made some people wince and hold their ears.

Bo heard the roaring as he pulled on shoulder pads in

At Auburn Bo rarely fumbled—a common flaw among flashy running backs. They carry the ball away from their bodies. Bo knew instinctively to tuck the ball close to his side.
Photo courtesy of Auburn University.

the Auburn dressing room under the stands. "I've never seen you work as hard as you worked for this game," Little Train James said.

Bo grinned. "I want to show that Alabama coach that I didn't come to Auburn to lose to 'Bama for four years."

Alabama jumped out to a 7–0 lead. Auburn crunched its way up the field and slammed across the goal line to tie the game, 7–7.

Players crashed into each other. Helmets butted helmets. Pads cracked against pads, the sound as sharp as rifle shots. Roaring filled the bowl. But the players heard only the "un-uh-un-uh" panting of twenty-two huge and muscled players.

Alabama crept ahead. As the fourth period began, the Crimson Tide led by eight points, 22–14.

Bo had ripped through tacklers to gain almost 5 yards a run. But when he tried to race to the side and skirt the end for a long run, Tide tacklers met him and knocked him down. His longest gain had been for only 12 yards.

"Go, Bo, Go," chanted Auburn fans.

Auburn had the ball on its 34, a long 66 yards from a touchdown. Auburn quarterback Randy Campbell pitched to Bo, who sprinted for the sideline. Two bulky defenders waited for him, arms outstretched.

An Auburn blocker knocked one tackler aside. Bo stepped left, drawing the other defender left, then burst by him on his right, the tackler clawing at empty air. "He seemed to explode past me," the 'Bama defender said later.

Bo raced up the sideline past the 50 . . . past the 40 . . . past the 30. . . . Then a lone 'Bama safety veered toward him. He leaped like a rocket at Bo to make a flying tackle.

Bo braked to a stop. The safety flew by him—a rocket shooting wide of its target.

That stop gave two Alabama backs time to catch up with Bo. They caught him from behind at the Alabama 13.

That 53-yard dash put Auburn within striking distance

of the touchdown it needed so badly to shorten the 8-point 'Bama lead.

But 'Bama's line threw back Bo's attempt and two other Auburn lunges toward the goal line. Auburn had to settle for a 3-point field goal. Auburn now trailed, 22–17. It still needed a touchdown to win.

A little later Auburn smashed to the Alabama 45. Fourth down, 1 yard to go for a first down. Should Auburn punt? If Auburn tried to get that yard and failed, Alabama would be only 55 yards away from the touchdown that would clinch victory.

Coach Dye signaled: Go for it! In the huddle Randy called the play. "Number 45 . . . Bo over the top . . ."

'Bama's defenders bunched up in the middle. They knew Auburn would hurtle Bo at them. "Stop Bo on this play," panting Tide defenders told one another, "and we win."

"Three . . . three . . ." Randy shouted the signals. He took the snap, spun, and rammed the ball into Bo's hands.

Bo ran toward a writhing wall of white and red jerseys. He leaped over helmets—and plunged downward one and a half yards away. First down!

The Tigers pushed to the Alabama 14. Alabama bunched up once more to stop Bo, figuring he would try to bullet to the goal line. Randy took the snap from the center, spun, and thrust the ball toward Bo. Bo dashed into the line—without the ball.

Randy gripped the ball in his right hand. He looked toward the goal line. He saw Bo curl toward the sideline. Randy flipped a pass. Bo reached out two large hands and snared the ball. He twisted toward the goal line. A 'Bama back pulled him to the ground at the 1-yard line.

Auburn stood a yard away from beating Alabama for the first time in ten years.

Alabama made a gallant last stand. Its line threw back three Auburn attempts to score. Now it was the fourth down with a yard to go for a winning touchdown and only seconds left in the game.

The game's winner or loser would be decided on this last play. In the huddle Randy called the play everyone knew he would call: "Number 45 . . . Bo over the top . . ."

Auburn and 'Bama fans sat suddenly silent, the drama of this moment hushing the afternoon's roaring.

Randy called the signals. "Two . . . two . . ."

Bo rushed forward and grabbed the ball. He soared high into the air. Arms, hands, and shoulders smacked him backward. Bo looked down through a forest of legs. He saw the white goal line. He knew what he had to do to prove an Alabama coach wrong.

Bo wiggled like a snake. He thrust out his hands that gripped the football.

Up shot a referee's arms. *Touchdown!*

Millions watching on TV across Alabama leaped into the air. Other millions slumped in their seats.

Auburn had won. The Tigers stood first in the state of Alabama. And a coach's prediction—that Bo would lose to Alabama for four years—had proven wrong.

SLUGGER

"Strike one!"

Bo shook his head. The fastball had swerved directly over the plate. He should have swung at it.

The University of Georgia pitcher wound up. In darted another fastball. It hummed straight down the middle. Bo swung. The ball smacked into the catcher's mitt.

"Strike two!" bellowed the umpire.

Bo bit his lower lip. He'd swung too late, "like a rusty gate," as the hitters say.

The pitcher wound up and threw another fastball. Bo swung. The ball smacked into the catcher's mitt.

"Strike three! Yer out!"

Bo walked glumly back to the Auburn bench. He had stepped up to the plate twenty-one times in this spring 1983 baseball season. And he had struck out all twenty-one times.

The Auburn baseball coach, Hal Baird, had once pitched in the big leagues. He reminded Bo that Bo had missed preseason baseball practice because he had been running on the track team. "You just have to swing a little quicker, Bo, and that will come with practice," Coach Baird said.

The track coach, Mel Rosen, had told Bo that he could

make next year's Olympic team as a sprinter. Earlier in the spring, Bo had sprinted across the finish line to become the only freshman to qualify for the National Collegiate Athletic Association (NCAA) 60-yard dash final. His times, 6.18 seconds for the 60-yard dash and 10.39 for the 100 meters, were among the fastest in the South.

When track season ended, Bo pulled on a baseball uniform. Baseball was still his second favorite sport. And playing baseball meant he was excused from the exhausting spring football drills. Other players grumbled louder about Bo being coach's pet. Coach Dye explained that Bo couldn't play baseball and football at the same time. But the grumbling grew louder.

Bo hated football practice but loved baseball practice. "Baseball practice," he once explained, "means you just run a couple of sprints and take a round of outfield practice catching flies and throwing to bases. Then you take a few rounds of batting practice, run a few sprints, and you're through. What I like best is that in baseball practice you go at your own pace."

During the next week, Bo took extra rounds of batting practice. In the next game he banged out two hits.

Coach Baird's eyes lit up when Bo hit one ball that flew over a distant light tower. And the coach shook his head, amazed, when Bo hit a ground ball to the second baseman and ran so fast that he beat the throw to first. Bo's batting average climbed from .000 to over .250.

The coach timed Bo running from home plate to first. Bo's time, racing from the right side of the plate, was 3.8 seconds. That was a half second faster, the coach said, than the major league average for hitters running from the left side, which is a step closer to first.

Auburn went to Tuscaloosa to play Alabama, a team Bo still relished beating. Before the game, two ruddy-faced men sat on the hood of a truck, drinking beer. The truck was parked near the outfield fence. The men remembered Bo's last-minute touchdown that beat Alabama's Crimson Tide.

33

As a baseball hitter, Bo impressed his coach, Hal Baird, almost
from the first day he swung a bat. "I have never seen anyone,"
Baird said, "who could run, throw, or hit for power the way Bo can."
Photo courtesy of Auburn University.

34

They began to taunt Bo. "You're no ballplayer, boy," they chanted, emphasizing the last word. They laughed derisively.

Bo smiled but said nothing. He struck out on his first at-bat. "Boy, you're really no ballplayer!" the men shouted louder.

Bo struck out the next time up. "Boy, you're a terrible ballplayer!"

Bo came up again in the seventh inning. From the fence the two beer drinkers yelled, "Hey, boy, hey boy!" Many people were laughing.

The Alabama pitcher threw a fastball. Bo swung, his long, muscled arms effortlessly sweeping the bat into the ball.

The ball soared toward that distant truck. The two men sat paralyzed, watching the ball streak toward them. At the last instant they dived off the truck's hood. The ball crashed into the hood with a loud clang that echoed across the ballpark.

Bo rounded the bases. The crowd sat stunned and silent. The red-faced men climbed into the truck and drove away.

Bo had decided to study family and child development. He took courses on how children grow and learn. He studied how a father and a mother can become a model for a child to learn from.

When a professor asked a question, Bo often stammered or stuttered the answer. To relax in class, Bo tried nibbling on paper straws, the kind he picked up by the dozens at McDonald's and other fast-food places.

Bo chewed out a straw every fifteen to twenty minutes. "I go quicker when I'm nervous," he told a friend. "Like yesterday I walked into a health class and found out we had a test. It had slipped my mind. I went through one straw in two minutes." He showed the friend a straw he had just been nibbling on. It looked like a cowboy's spurs.

His best friend, Lionel "Little Train" James, asked Bo to come to parties with him in the evenings. Bo usually said no. He stayed in the room to study. "I am not the guy who gets the best grades in my class," he told someone. "But I don't get the lowest grades either. I've got a C average, but I'd like to do better."

At night Bo liked to listen to Mahalia Jackson gospel records. "I don't leave my records out by the stereo," he told another friend. Bo worried that his gospel records might get mixed up with Little Train's Gap Band and Prince records—loud rock 'n' roll that made Bo wince.

Bo's idea of a great Saturday night was a visit to the video arcade on College Street. There he played games for hours; the kind of games, he said, "where you're dodging bullets all the time."

One evening he came out of the arcade and realized he had stayed too long. A parking ticket clung to the windshield of the car he had borrowed from a friend.

Bo drove to the police station and paid the fine. "It's a fifty-cent fine," he told another player later. "But if you don't pay it within twenty-four hours, it goes up to a dollar."

Once the lawbreaker, Bo now obeyed all the laws.

The hot sun beat down on the Auburn football players, who were dressed only in shorts and sneakers. For the past two hours, in 90-degree heat, the players had labored through dozens of exercises. Now they were trudging to the weight room to pick up loads as heavy as 400 pounds.

"I notice Bo doesn't have to go to the weight room," one player said. "At practices Bo gets away with murder."

Coach Dye heard the grumbling. He knew he and his assistant coaches had let up on Bo. The coaches couldn't risk Bo leaving the team. This 1983 team, the coach sensed, could win its first Southeastern Conference championship in more than ten years. But it was just another team without Bo.

As a student at Auburn, Bo majored in child development. But he showed interest in other fields like archeology, inspecting here an ancient vase. "I enjoy being a student, taking notes, going to classes," he said. "In classes I am just another Auburn student."
Photo: Bill Harris.

On the other hand, Auburn's angry players might not block for Bo. When Bo got the ball, they might let up and Bo would be flattened by an avalanche of tacklers.

The coach wondered what he should do.

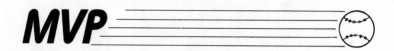

MVP

"We got a bet, Bo," Pat Washington reminded Bo. "And you're going to lose the bet."

"No way I'm going to lose," Bo said, smiling.

Pat and Bo stood on the pitcher's mound of the Auburn baseball field. Pat was Auburn's number one passer. Bo had told Pat that he could throw a football longer than Pat. The passer laughed. Pat knew he could throw a ball farther.

"You throw first, Pat," Bo said.

Pat gripped the ball, ran forward, and threw. The ball came down about 20 yards short of the fence, which was 107 yards away.

Bo gripped another football. He ran forward and let it fly. The ball seemed to take off as though shot from a gun. Pat stared. The ball thudded into the ground just short of the fence—a 100-yard throw that won the bet for Bo. He had beaten Pat at what Pat did best—throwing a football.

"I'm not surprised," baseball coach Hal Baird said when he heard of Bo's throw. "We have a radar gun that checks the speed of balls thrown by our pitchers. We know that big league pitchers have been clocked throwing 92 to 93 miles an hour with that gun. One day Bo walked to the mound and without even a warm-up pitch, he threw the ball at 90 miles an hour. He had thrown a major league fastball—without even a warm-up."

A player could be heard throwing up. Pale faces stared at the whitewashed walls, faces taut with tension. The Auburn quarterback paced the room, fists clenched, as he mumbled the numbers of plays he had memorized.

In an hour the Auburn football team would run out onto the field for the first game of the 1983 season. Players wondered: How will I do? Will I mess up? Will we lose?

Bo stretched out on the floor of the locker room, dressed in football shoes and pants, bare to the waist. He yawned. He turned on his side, his bulging arms forming a pillow.

"Look!" said a freshman tackle. "Bo's falling asleep!"

"He likes to do that," a senior said. "Bo never gets the jitters."

Bo's figure stretched six feet two in length across the stone floor. His 222-pound body had the sculpted hardness of black marble. Other players, their bodies hard and muscular, looked at Bo's body with wonder in their eyes. "He never lifts weights, he never does situps and pushups. But look at all that strength. Where does it come from?"

Bo had a ready answer, learned from his mother: "God's blessings."

Auburn won that game, beating Southern Mississippi. Bo rampaged for 73 yards in only 11 carries. The next week, however, Texas beat Auburn, 20–7. Bo gained only 35 yards but he got the ball only 7 times. "What a mistake," Coach Dye admitted after the game. "We got the best runner in the conference and he gets the ball only seven times. That mistake won't happen again."

Nor did it. The Tigers ripped through their next eight opponents, beating them all. Bo gained 123 yards against Florida State, another 123 against Georgia Tech, and 196 against a huge University of Florida team.

The 9-won, 1-lost Tigers came down to their final

game—against Alabama in the Iron Bowl at Legion Field in Birmingham. Bo didn't fall asleep before that game.

"Bo takes it easy in practice all season," one player said. "But he sure worked hard to get ready for this game today."

"I'll tell you," said another player, "it used to bother me, Bo getting the easy treatment from the coaches. But it doesn't bother me any more. Because on game day Bo is always ready."

Coach Dye heard that and had to smile. His worries about treating Bo in a special way had vanished.

Bo streaked for two touchdowns against 'Bama, whose assistant coach had said Bo couldn't start on the team until his junior year. A sophomore now, he ran 69 yards for one touchdown and 71 yards for a second. All told, he gained 256 yards against the Tide. Auburn won. For the second straight season, Bo got the award as the game's Most Valuable Player.

In that 1983 season Bo had gained 7.7 yards a carry. Nebraska's Mike Rozier, a college senior, had gained 7.8 yards a carry—and that had helped him to win the Heisman Trophy as the nation's number one player. Football writers named Rozier and Bo to their All-American teams. Many writers predicted that Bo would win the Heisman as a junior in 1984. Only a small handful of juniors, Herschel Walker among them, had won the Heisman.

Auburn had captured its first Southeastern Conference (SEC) championship in more than a decade. As the SEC champion, it went to the Sugar Bowl in New Orleans to play Michigan, the Big Ten Conference champion.

Bo flashed through Michigan tacklers to average almost 6 yards a gain. But Little Train James banged up the middle on one bruising run after another to keep Auburn in the game. Auburn beat Michigan in the Sugar Bowl, 9–7.

After the game an official handed Bo a trophy "You were picked as the game's Most Valuable Player," the official said. "Congratulations!"

40

"Thanks," Bo said. "But I wasn't the game's most valuable player." Bo walked across the dressing room and handed the trophy to Little Train.

A reporter asked Bo, "Which sport do you like better, football or baseball?"

"Football is intense," Bo said. "Baseball's more relaxed. But there's more concentration in baseball, so I like it better than football. You don't have to concentrate to knock the stuffing out of somebody on a football field."

"Will you play centerfield again for Auburn next spring, or will you try to be a pitcher? Hal Baird says you have the fastball of a big league pitcher."

"I am not going to play baseball next spring," Bo said.

WANTED

The gun's blast echoed in the humid air. Six sprinters lunged out of the starting blocks at the Florida Relays. Bo, in the middle, heard the crunch of dirt under flying spikes. Faces contorted, arms swinging, legs rising and falling like the pistons of a powerful engine, Bo drove for the finish line almost 100 meters away.

Bo drew ahead. He flashed across the finish line. Moments later, gasping, with sweat streaming down his face, he looked up at the infield clock and saw his time: 10.39 seconds.

That was the seventh fastest 100 meters ever run by an Auburn sprinter. But Bo knew that the time was not good enough to push him where he wanted to go next— to the tryouts for the 1984 Olympic team.

Bo had given up baseball in the spring of 1984 to try to make the Olympic team. Since his third grade days, track had been his favorite sport. He still looked with pride on the two trophies he had won as state decathlon champion. In college he had flown over 40 yards in 4.12 seconds, faster than anyone on the Auburn football team. Herschel Walker had run the 40 in 4.30 seconds. Bo's time, according to *Sports Illustrated* magazine, was the fastest every clocked by a college player. But as Bo knew, there was no 40-yard dash in the Olympics.

"Bo could have been an Olympic sprinter," track coach Mel Rosen said. "But he had to concentrate on football in the fall and that cost him the practice time he needed."

Baseball scouts came to Auburn to talk to Bo. They still remembered the high school pitcher and slugger whom the Yankees had offered $250,000. "He was awesome in high school," scout Ken Gonzales told the Kansas City Royals. "I was always kind of afraid he would hurt somebody because he threw so fast and hit the ball so hard."

But Bo had missed a year of college baseball. That kind of baseball had prepped stars like Tom Seaver and Bo's idol, Reggie Jackson, for the big leagues. Baseball scouts wondered: Could Bo again show the glowing promise he had flashed in high school?

"IS BO GOING?"

Auburn football fans stared with worry on their faces at that headline. A new pro football league, the United States Football League (USFL), had started. It had already lured Herschel Walker out of college with bagfuls of money. Now a USFL team, the Birmingham Stallions, was offering Bo a half million dollars to quit Auburn and play for them.

No, Bo said. He told the Stallions of his ambition to be the first in his family to get a college degree.

"You must be crazy," Bo's teammates said. "How could you turn down all that money?"

"Money can't buy happiness," Bo said. "I know what it feels like to be poor. But I want to play where I will find the most happiness—in college, at Auburn."

"But you can live The Dream," a black athlete told Bo. The Dream, to many young blacks, was escaping the ghetto riding atop a football or basketball or baseball. Then you could live The Dream—a house in the suburbs, a car, a loving family.

43

"No, I don't follow any dream," Bo said. "Bo's going to follow his heart."

Bo had learned a trick to erase the stutter when he used the word "I." It often came out as "I-I-I-I." So he said it as seldom as he could. Instead he referred to himself in the third person, as "Bo."

Auburn began its 1984 season by facing the University of Miami in the Kickoff Classic, a game played annually between two of the previous season's best teams. Bo blasted through the Miami line to gain almost 5 yards a run. Midway through the game a tackler grabbed his ankle and twisted it. Bo limped off the field but he came back to finish the game. Miami eked out a 20–18 victory.

Auburn next played Texas.

Bo limped at practice, pain shooting from the twisted ankle. But he wanted to play against Texas, the only team to beat Auburn in 1983. Early in the game he smashed across for a touchdown. An Auburn player noticed his limp. "If you're in pain, don't play," the player told Bo. "People get injured when they try to play in pain. You can't go all out and escape being hurt."

But with the game tied, Bo wanted to score and put Auburn in the lead. A little later Bo shot around left end and raced up the sideline. A Texas safety, Jerry Gray, raced after Bo, but when Bo got ahead of anyone, he never was caught from behind.

Now his ankle throbbed with pain. Bo slowed up. Gray dived at Bo and caught him around the knees. Bo dropped to the ground like a chopped tree.

His right shoulder banged into the turf. Bo got up slowly, feeling the shoulder. It felt strange, kind of stiff.

Bo played a few more minutes. By then the shoulder ached. Bo walked to the dressing room. A trainer cut off his jersey and unbuckled his shoulder pads.

Bo looked at the trainer. Worry showed on Bo's face. Was the shoulder hurt badly? The trainer said he didn't know.

Texas won, 35–27, and the Auburn Tigers flew back home.

That night doctors X-rayed the shoulder. "The shoulder is separated, Bo," the doctors said. "We are going to have to operate on it."

"Will I play again—"

"Probably not this season."

That night Bo tossed and turned in a hospital bed. He had never been seriously hurt in his life. Now, he realized, one play could end an athlete's career. Suppose he had twisted a knee? His knees were the wheels that had carried him to All-America honors in football, to trophies in track, and to a quarter-of-a-million-dollar offer in baseball. Damaged knees would mean that Bo would be just another runner, just another face in the crowd.

He should never have played with that sore ankle. He had no business being out there on that field. Now all his ambitions—the Heisman, being first in the pro football draft, setting rushing records at Auburn—might be blown away.

That night, as Bo said later without any shame, "I cried like a baby."

LINDA

"Got no Heisman last year, did you, Bo?"

Bo smiled at the spectator who had shot that needle at him. Bo was tossing a ball to a teammate near the Auburn dugout at the University of Georgia's Foley Stadium. More than three thousand people, a large crowd for a college baseball game, filled the stands for this spring 1985 night game.

Georgia fans still wore joy on their faces when they talked of how Herschel Walker had won the Heisman in 1982. This Bo Jackson was no Herschel Walker—and the fans were going to remind him of that all during this baseball game.

Indeed, the 1984 football season had been disappointing for Bo and Auburn. He had been expected to win the Heisman. Instead, Boston College's Doug Flutie won it. True, Bo had surprised doctors by coming back to play in that 1984 season after being out of action for six weeks. In half a season he gained 5.5 yards a run, well below his 7.7 average a year earlier. He had scored only 5 touchdowns, compared to 12 a year earlier. The Tigers, losers of only one game in 1983, lost four in 1984, including a 17–15 heartbreaker to Alabama, the Tide's first victory over Bo.

The Tigers went to the Liberty Bowl and beat Arkansas, 21–15. It was Bo's third straight bowl triumph. The

Tigers had beaten Boston College after his freshman year, Michigan after his sophomore year. And for the second straight bowl game, Bo was selected as the game's Most Valuable Player—an honor that this time he kept.

His Olympic hopes ended, Bo decided to give up track in the spring of 1985 and concentrate on baseball. He was determined to make up for his disappointments in track and football in 1984 by blazing a sensational 1985 baseball season.

And so far it had been sensational. Bo was batting close to .400. He had slugged a dozen home runs. But when he struck out during his first at-bat here at Foley Stadium, a few Georgia fans let him know he was no Herschel Walker who had won the Heisman.

Bo turned to a teammate and said, laughing, "The way I get back at people like that is this—I take it out on the baseball."

Bo batted again in the third inning. The Georgia pitcher twisted off a curve. Bo caught the curveball "hanging"—it didn't swerve away, as good curves should. Bo met the ball with those huge arms fully extended—a picture-perfect slugger's swing.

The ball soared through the night toward the shadowy centerfield fence. Spectators rose slowly, hushed, hypnotized by the ball's seemingly endless flight. The ball shot high over the fence at the 375-foot mark. Still rising, it struck the top of an 85-foot-high light tower.

"It was," said coach Hal Baird, a big league veteran, "the hardest hit ball I have ever seen."

The taunts had died in people's throats. As Bo rounded second base, a roar rose steadily into the night. People stood and applauded the longest home run they had ever seen hit.

Bo kept them on their feet. He slammed two more home runs that night. When he came to bat for the last time and slugged a double, he heard boos—the Georgia fans had hoped he'd hit a fourth straight home run.

His muscled arms swinging the bat as though it were a toothpick, Bo awaits a pitch. Bo can bench press more than 400 pounds, even though he rarely works out with weights. He never does situps or pushups. Photo: Bill Harris.

"I'll tell you how good a baseball player Bo is," Coach Baird said to reporters after the game. "I have seen three or four other guys who can run like he can. I have seen three or four guys who can throw like he can. I have seen three or four guys who could hit for power like he can.

But those were twelve different people. It sounds like I'm talking about Superman."

Big league scouts agreed that Bo was special. Major League scout Dick Egan told other scouts, "He's got as much talent as Mickey Mantle or Willie Mays."

Baseball wanted him—but baseball scouts knew they would have to fight football scouts to get him. Kansas City Chiefs' scout Les Miller said, "He has that rare potential to be one of the all-time greats in football."

Could Bo star in pro football *and* baseball? For the first time, during that spring of 1985, sportswriters asked that question. The writers pointed out that no one had ever starred in both sports. Olympic champion Jim Thorpe had tried way back before World War I. Thorpe became a Hall of Fame football player—but he rode the bench in baseball with the old New York Giants. More recently, All-American passer John Elway tried baseball—but went back to football.

"I wish I could do both," Bo said. "At least I'd like to try both. But there is always going to be somebody to say, 'No, he can't do it,' " He smiled. "You know, sometimes I like to make people look a little foolish."

Bo sat on the floor, facing the children. They came each week to the Auburn Child Study Center. Bo and other child development majors came to the Center to talk to boys and girls about their problems. Some children said their parents didn't love them. Other parents were drug addicts. Some children came to seek advice.

"They need someone to teach them right from wrong," Bo told a friend one day.

"Bo is sincere," Janice Grover, one of the Center's faculty, said to a visitor. "He has a real concern for children as people. He makes it a point to get down to their eye level to talk to them."

She smiled. "And Bo is the one who volunteers to sweep the floor after all the kids are gone."

49

Church and youth clubs began to invite Bo to come to their dinners and meetings to speak. He always said yes.

"Don't run life too fast," he told teenagers. "You only have one life. You'll either end up in jail somewhere serving time or you'll be dead. Obey your parents."

He told the kids how wild he had been as a teenager—a bully, a thief. He told how he once stole money from his mother's purse, money she needed to pay an insurance bill.

"My life then is not the way you should live your life. Don't get mixed up with drugs and youth gangs the way I did. Don't ever have your mom say you'll end up in a penitentiary before you're twenty-one, which is where I was headed."

After listening to one of Bo's talks, Cheryl Deaton, principal of an Auburn school, told a reporter: "Bo really does make a special effort to be with the kids, to be a role model. Not to be a hero and a big man, but to be somebody for them to look up to.

"The kids can listen to us all day long, and it doesn't sink in. But when they see somebody as famous as Bo sitting down with them—he sits with them, he doesn't stand up and lecture—and taking the time to talk with them . . . well, rapture is a good word to describe the way they look."

It was the summer of 1985. School had ended. That summer, as he had during the previous two summers, Bo drove each morning into Birmingham, where he worked as a clerk at the Colonial Bank. He had saved up the money he'd earned at the bank to buy a 1983 Oldsmobile Cutlass.

The phone in Bo's dormitory room rang often. The callers were Auburn women who wondered if Bo might like to go to a movie or a picnic or for a stroll around campus. Bo always said no to those uninvited calls.

"There are a lot of people who are trouble people," he said. "They want to be seen with somebody famous because then people will think they are important. I stay away from those kind of people."

He danced—not too well, either—at parties where the football players danced with girls. But he usually left early. And he always left alone or with Little Train or one of his friends. He never left alone with a girl.

But he had been eyeing a young woman who attended child development classes with Bo. The woman's name was Linda Garrett and she was majoring in child psychology.

She and Bo began to go out on dates. Often they drove to a fast-food restaurant—Bo loved them all—for Cokes and burgers. His friends spotted them. They told Bo that Linda looked like Tina Turner.

Bo told Linda about some of the weird things that happened to him now that he was gaining fame. One day he rammed a car that stopped suddenly in front of him.

A woman jumped out of the other car and snapped at him, "What's your name?"

"Bo Jackson."

The woman stared, startled, and then said in a caring voice, "Are you all right?"

A few weeks later Auburn played Tennessee. Just before the game Bo got a note from the woman. It read: "Smash Tennessee like you smashed my car."

Linda laughed at the story. Like other child development majors, she had been touched by Bo's open affection for children.

A few days later, Bo showed Linda another letter to him. The letter came from a woman who wanted his autograph. Bo's autograph, she wrote, could save a teenage boy's life.

HAPPINESS

Fourteen-year-old Jon Greenwood swung his bike leftward. He didn't see the station wagon curve into his path. When Jon awoke two days later in an Anniston, Alabama, hospital, doctors told him they had amputated his right leg.

The slim, blue-eyed Jon refused to eat, angered by a fate that would take a leg away from an athlete. His weight sunk from 130 to 90 pounds.

His dietician, Cindy Templeton, knew that Jon idolized Bo Jackson. "If I get you Bo's autograph, Jon," she asked the teenager, "will you start to eat the way you must to live?"

Jon nodded glumly. Why would Bo Jackson send an autograph to a boy in Anniston?

Cindy, an Auburn graduate, wrote to Bo and asked for his autograph. She asked that Bo send the autograph to Jon at his Anniston home.

A few days later Jon's phone rang.

"Jon Greenwood?" the caller's voice asked.

"Yes."

"Do you know anyone at Auburn?"

"I only know one person at Auburn. That's Bo Jackson."

"You're talking to him."

Jon stared at the phone, not believing what he had just heard. But within a minute Bo convinced Jon that he indeed was talking to the real Bo Jackson.

Bo told Jon he had to eat to get strong and well again. If Jon did eat, Bo promised, Bo would send a surprise.

Two days later a special-delivery package arrived. Jon opened the package. To Jon's delight, he saw photographs of Bo—personally autographed by Bo to Jon Greenwood. "That," Jon told his mother, "sure was some surprise."

Early the next morning Jon's grandmother told him to roll his wheelchair toward the driveway. As Jon got near the driveway, he saw a car pull up. He saw Cindy sitting in the back seat next to a broad-shouldered man who looked like—

Bo Jackson bounded out of the car. "What you doing, man?" he shouted at Jon. He extended a hand to the gaping Jon.

For the next hour, Bo talked to Jon about football and fishing. Later Bo told a friend, "He knows I care. I told him he can't sit and feel sorry for himself. You got to get up and do things even if you don't want to do them."

"Bo cares," Jon told his friends back in Anniston. "He had to care or he wouldn't have come."

"Bo?"

"Yes, this is Bo Jackson."

Calling on Bo this summer afternoon in 1985 was an official of baseball's California Angels. He told Bo that the Angels had been impressed by Bo's baseball record the previous spring. Bo had hit .401 and rapped 17 home runs. He had scored 55 runs, the most of any Auburn player. He had stolen 9 bases in 10 tries.

In the 1985 baseball draft a few days earlier, the Angels had drafted Bo. The Yankees, who had failed to sign Bo, had lost the rights to him.

The Angels official asked Bo to sign with the Angels. Bo would play for a minor league team in 1985, perhaps with the Angels in 1986. "We'll give you a lot of money,"

53

the official said. "And this fall you can go back to Auburn to study for your degree."

Bo said no to a lot of money for the third time. If he took the money, he told the official, he could not play football that fall. And Bo still wanted to win the Heisman and set a record for rushing at Auburn.

Later, an Angel official, Larry Himes, told a reporter: "Bo will never know how much money we might have offered him. He owns all the stuff to be a great All-Star baseball player. He's really exciting."

Bo shrugged when reporters asked him why he had chosen no-pay college football over high-pay big league baseball. "I have to go where I am happiest. And happiness right now is winning the SEC championship for Auburn."

Now a senior, Bo knew this season would be his last chance to win the Heisman and set the yardage record at Auburn. To help Bo set that record, Coach Dye changed the Tiger offense. He switched from the wishbone backfield formation to the I formation. In the wishbone, any one of three backs can run with the ball. In the I, the tailback runs with the ball on most plays. Bo would be Auburn's tailback.

Auburn opened the 1985 season by blowing away Southeast Louisiana, 49–7. Bo gained 290 yards, his most ever, and scored 4 touchdowns.

The next week he streaked 205 yards and scored 2 touchdowns as Auburn beat Southern Mississippi, 29–18.

The Tigers went to Knoxville to play Tennessee. Early in the second half a tackler cut down Bo. He rose slowly and limped out of the game. His knee ached. He remembered how he had tried to run on a sore ankle against Texas. A tackler had caught him from behind and almost wrecked his career. Bo had learned his lesson. He would not play again while hurt. He stayed out of the game and Auburn lost, 38–20.

Sportswriters scolded him in their columns. They asked: Was Bo a quitter? Many were among the one thousand-odd writers and broadcasters who picked the Heis-

54

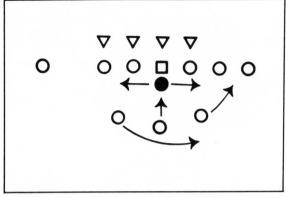

Diagram shows the wishbone formation that Auburn used during Bo's first three seasons. From the wishbone, the quarterback (dark circle) can run left or right or he can pitch the ball to any one of his three running backs. Any one of the four backfield players can carry the ball.

Diagram: Barbara Devaney.

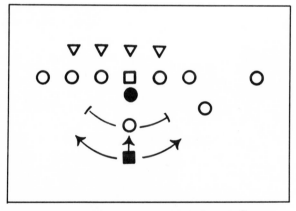

Diagram of the I formation, which Coach Dye installed for Bo's last season, shows two deep backs behind the quarterback (dark circle): the blocking back and the tailback (dark square). From the I formation the quarterback, on running plays, nearly always gives the ball to the tailback. Bo, the tailback, became the number-one ball carrier and leading rusher.

Diagram: Barbara Devaney.

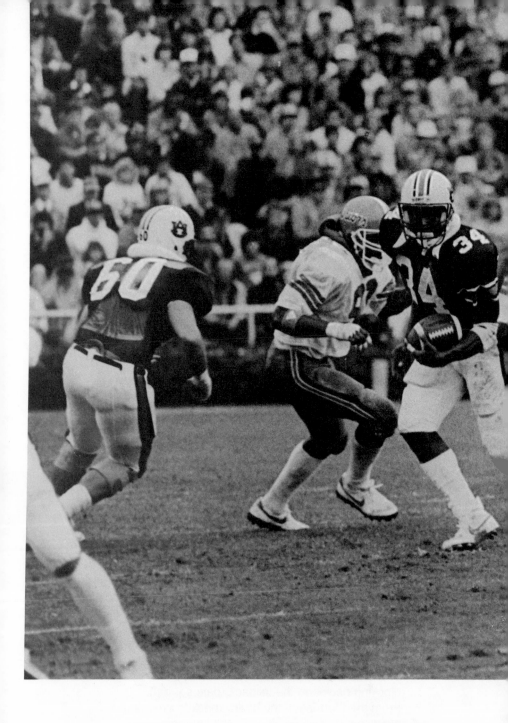

Bo weaves through the Florida line as he begins the 1985 season in pursuit of the Heisman. Each day, on his way to classes, he passed the Heisman won in 1971 by Auburn quarterback Pat

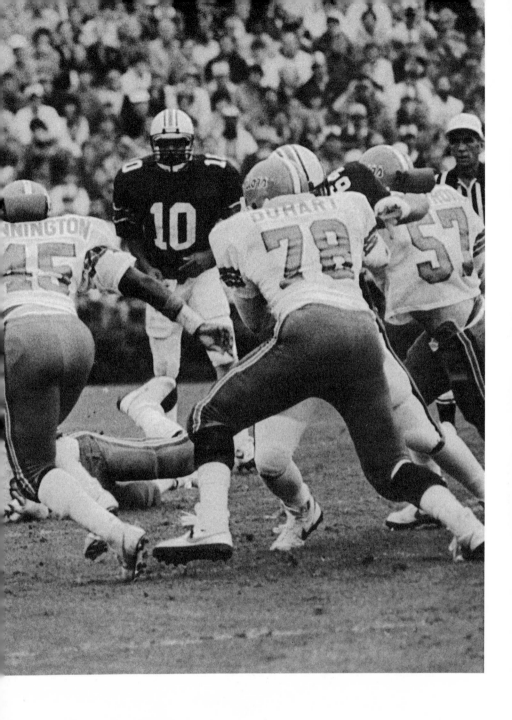

Sullivan. That trophy—and questions from reporters—reminded him
that his college career would end in frustration if he failed to win the
Heisman. Photo courtesy of Wide World.

man winner. They asked themselves: Should a player who refused to play in pain be awarded the Heisman?

Bo came back the next week to score 2 touchdowns as Auburn beat Mississippi, 41–0. He scored 2 more touchdowns as Auburn overwhelmed Florida State, 59–27. He sprinted 76 yards to the winning touchdown as Auburn narrowly beat Georgia Tech, 17–14. He gained 6 yards a try and scored 2 touchdowns as Auburn beat Mississippi State, 21–9.

During a scrimmage the next week, a teammate's helmet rammed into Bo's thigh. "A badly bruised thigh," a trainer told Coach Dye. Bo tried to play that Saturday

The number-one candidate for the Heisman Trophy in 1985, Bo was surrounded by microphones after each Tiger game. The reporters always asked: Did he think he would win the Heisman? Bo heard the question so often that it irritated him. His typical answer was "I hope so, but that's up to the people who vote for the Heisman." Photo: Bill Harris.

against Florida. But in the first two periods he gained only 48 yards in 16 tries. He hobbled off the field. He knew he could do no good for Auburn and a lot of harm to himself. Auburn lost, 14–10.

Again Bo's critics said that he had quit. Many writers and broadcasters said they doubted they would pick Bo for the Heisman.

Bo's teammates shook their heads when they read what columnists wrote about Bo. "He's human like everybody else," defensive back Kevin Porter said. "He's got bones that break; he's got muscles that bruise."

Each day Bo walked through the Auburn athletic building. He passed the Heisman Trophy that had been won by Auburn quarterback Pat Sullivan in 1971.

Bo tried not to think about the Heisman. He told people he didn't care whether he won the Heisman or not. He knew no one believed him.

"All I can say is that I am not a quitter," he told reporters. "If I felt it was necessary to take myself out of competition, it is not because I am a coward."

He paused. "But maybe now I have to go out and prove myself all over again."

HEISMAN

Quarterback Pat Washington hunched over the center. He called the signals. He saw the huge Georgia defenders—the ferocious "Dawgs," as they called themselves—bunch up to stop Bo. They guessed that Bo would come hurtling at them from the tailback spot.

Pat took the snap and spun. He pitched the ball to Bo, who sprinted toward the left side. Bo grabbed the ball—and suddenly stopped.

He whirled and sped toward the right sideline. Surprised Dawgs stumbled as they tried to stop and turn. Bo shot through a hole between two off-balance defenders. Two safeties rushed up to stop him.

Bo spun and now sped back toward the left sideline. This was now a footrace to a finish line—that left sideline. His breath coming in hard gasps—"un-uh-un-uh"—Bo got to the sideline one straining arm's length ahead of the safeties. Bo hung a sharp right turn and sped untouched down the sideline—a 67-yard touchdown run.

Bo knew this game against Georgia—and his last regular-season game two weeks from now against Alabama—were his last chances "to prove himself all over again" and win the Heisman.

On this afternoon against Georgia, Bo raced for 2 touchdowns. He gained 121 yards in 19 carries—better than 6 yards a try. And Auburn beat Georgia, 24–10.

Bo rooted for his teammates who played defense when he came off the field. When Bo was tempted to leave Auburn to join the new league's Birmingham Stallions, teammates asked him to stay. "He knows what a great future he has in pro football," Coach Dye said, "but Bo wants to stay until he can graduate." Photo: Bill Harris.

Early in the second half of that game, a Dawg drove like a spear into Bo's chest. As Bo hit the ground, pain flared across his side. Bo said nothing and stayed in the game.

During the next two weeks the Tigers practiced for their final regular-season game—the annual Iron Bowl against Alabama. Bo's chest hurt. But he told himself that the pain would be gone within two weeks.

On the Monday before the 'Bama game, Bo went to bed early. He could not sleep. When he took a deep breath, pain knifed into his ribs.

The next day Bo visited Auburn's team physician, Dr.

61

Charles Veale. The doctor X-rayed Bo's ribs. A little later he told Bo, "You played the last half of that Georgia game with two broken ribs."

A frown creased Bo's large face. "Hey," he said to the doctor, "can we keep this a secret?"

Bo knew that newspapermen would say that he used the broken ribs to duck away from a tough foe like 'Bama. The Tide could make him look bad on national TV as the Heisman voting began.

Coach Dye ordered special shoulder pads for Bo. The pads would protect the broken ribs. But they could not be too padded. Bulky pads might tip off the Alabama players that a shot at Bo's ribs could knock him out of the game.

Bo knew he could play at full speed; by Saturday, the pain had gone. And what better way "to prove himself all over again" than to play well against Alabama?

In a packed Legion Field that Saturday, the roar of "Ro*llll* . . . Tide . . . ro*llll* . . ." mixed with that traditional roar from the other side: "Wa*rrrr* . . . Eagle . . . wa*rrrr* . . ."

"It was an Iron Bowl," Birmingham News sportswriter Wayne Hester wrote the next day, "that topped all Iron Bowls."

Alabama rushed out to a 13–0 lead. The 'Bama defenders hounded Bo. Whenever Bo touched a ball, wrote one reporter, "half the defense was sure to follow."

But Bo banged over people to gain 51 yards in his first 12 carries. Auburn drove deep enough into 'Bama territory to kick a field goal. A little later Bo slashed through the 'Bama line from the 7—Alabama 13, Auburn 10.

Alabama kicked a field goal to stretch its lead to 16–10. That was still the score as the final period began, Legion Field a bowl filled with deafening noise. Millions watched across the country as ABC-TV's Keith Jackson described the action.

The Tigers stood 80 yards away from the touchdown that would put them ahead. "We have to keep pushing and pushing," Bo told his teammates.

Bo caught a pass and dashed to the Auburn 30. He carried 6 more times for 41 yards. Auburn crunched to the Alabama 1. On fourth down Bo dived into the end zone—Auburn 17, Alabama 16.

Alabama stormed back to score. Alabama tried for a two-point conversion and failed—Alabama 22, Auburn 17.

"Keep driving, keep driving," Bo told his teammates. They had the ball at the Auburn 30, 70 yards from the touchdown that would put them ahead.

With Bo as their spearhead, Auburn drove from their 30 to the Alabama end zone in two minutes. Auburn tried for a two-point conversion and failed. But with only 57 seconds left, Auburn led, 23–22.

Racing the clock, 'Bama quarterback Mike Shula steered his team to the Auburn 40. There was time left for only one more play. Alabama sent in its field goal kicker to try to boom the ball between the goal posts from 51 yards away. The ball was set down and kicked as the game's last second ticked off. The ball sailed between the uprights. A field goal, three points! Alabama had won this greatest Iron Bowl ever, 25–23.

Bo shook the hands of the 'Bama players. He had triumphed twice over the Tide; the Tide had triumphed twice over his Auburn team (the two Tide victories were taken by only four points, 17–15 and 25–23).

No one could call Bo a quitter when word spread the next day that Bo had played against Georgia and Alabama with broken ribs. "If anybody goes out into the Iron Bowl and plays with broken ribs," said Auburn tackle Steve Wallace, "if that's not courage, what is it?"

Bo had passed one goal line. In his career he had gained 4,303 yards, more than any runner in Auburn history, an average of 6.5 yards each time he ran with the ball. That had been his first goal as a freshman—to become Auburn's all-time greatest runner. His second goal had been to win the Heisman.

Had he proven himself all over again—this time to the voters for the Heisman?

DECISION

His heart beat like a hammer. It beat so loud he was sure the people in the next row could hear it.

Bo sat on a chair in a high-ceilinged room at New York City's Downtown Athletic Club. TV cameras stared at him and three other young men seated in a row, all dressed in business suits, shirts, and ties. They were Miami quarterback Vinnie Testaverde, Iowa quarterback Chuck Long, and Michigan State running back Lorenzo White.

The Downtown Athletic Club, which awards the Heisman, had asked the four to fly to New York early in December. The four had received the most votes for the 1985 Heisman Trophy. In a few minutes, while millions watched on TV, the winner would be announced.

Bo thought to himself that it would be hard if he came this close to grasping the trophy only to have to watch it slip into someone else's hands. Bo turned to Lorenzo White and said: "I don't get nervous even before a big game. I yawn and sleep. But right now here, I think my heart is going to jump out of my shirt."

A Downtown Athletic Club official stepped in front of the TV cameras. He said that the voting had been the closest in the 50-year history of the Heisman.

Then he announced the winner.

With his heart beating so loudly he was sure people in the second row could hear it, Bo watches apprehensively as a Downtown Athletic Club official comes forward to announce the 1985 Heisman winner. On Bo's left is Miami's Vinnie Testaverde, who won the award a year later. Michigan State's Lorenzo White is on Bo's right. Next to Lorenzo is Iowa quarterback Chuck Long, who finished second to Bo in the closest voting in the 51-year Heisman Trophy history. Photo courtesy of the Downtown Athletic Club.

About fifty of Bo's relatives and friends squeezed into the living room of the house of Bo's mother in Bessemer. Reporters and photographers stood in the doorways, watching. Bo's father and mother sat on chairs, looking at the flickering image of the official on a small black and white TV set.

"The 1985 Heisman Trophy winner," the man on the screen was saying, "is Bo Jackson!"

"*Allll* right, he did it!" one of Bo's sisters screamed. People jumped, clapped, whooped, shrieked. They shouted "Bo! Bo!" as Bo stepped up to receive the trophy.

Minutes later the phone rang. One of Bo's sisters picked it up. "Bo's on the phone, Mama!" she screamed. "Bo's on the phone!"

His mother smiled. She picked up the receiver. She heard her son say, "Hello, Mama, how's everything?"

Back in New York reporters wanted to know all about Bo. He talked of his life as a youth, how he stole and

Bo poses with the Heisman Trophy. The plaque on the trophy reads: "The Heisman Memorial Trophy is presented by Downtown Athletic Club of New York City to Vincent 'Bo' Jackson, Auburn University, as the Outstanding College Football Player in the United States for 1985." Photo courtesy of the Downtown Athletic Club.

bullied. He told how his mother, Dick Atchison, his religion, and sports had steered him to "the high road."

What is the real Bo like? reporters asked.

His favorite TV shows were "That's Incredible" and

"The Cosby Show," he said. His favorite food was liver. He hated spinach. His favorite sports were hunting and fishing.

Did he have a girlfriend?

He didn't like to talk about his intimate life. But, yes, there was a young woman back in Auburn. He dated her. He would not tell them her name.

He had hit .401 and 17 homers as a centerfielder for the baseball team. He had won the Heisman Trophy in football. Which sport would he pick as a pro career? "First of all," he said, "I want to get my college degree. When I finish with sports, I can always turn back to my academics and use my degree to get a job and further myself."

But which would it be, Bo? Baseball or football? "I am not going to decide what I am going to do until after next spring's baseball season."

Would he take the highest money offer? "I won't make my decision based on money. I know what it feels like to

At a press conference with Coach Pat Dye shortly after he won the Heisman, Bo shows reporters a cowboy hat and tells them, jokingly, that when the time comes to decide between football and baseball, he will toss the names of the two sports into a hat and draw one. Bo knew the decision would not be that easy. Photo courtesy of Wide World.

be poor, but money can't buy happiness. I just want to play where I'll find the most happiness."

Bo flew back to Auburn. He joined the football team as it prepared to meet Texas A & M on New Year's Day 1986 in the Cotton Bowl game in Dallas. In Bo's first three years at Auburn, the Tigers had gone to three straight bowl games and won all three. Bo was the MVP in two of them.

Bo was the MVP a third straight year at the 1986 Cotton Bowl. He gained 129 yards and rammed across for 2 touchdowns. But Texas A & M overpowered the Auburn defense to win, 36–16.

Bo began his last semester at Auburn in January of 1986. He would not get his degree in June, when his class graduated. But he would need only to complete three more courses to earn his degree, a goal for which he had given up offers of as much as a half million dollars.

"Being a student and going to the classroom, just another Auburn student, is the only time I can be just a face in the crowd," he told a reporter. "And that's the way I like it. I like going to class. I like taking notes and asking questions and trying to learn just like anybody else, nobody expecting me to do something great."

He and Linda, who were dating only each other now, talked about their future after school. Both wanted to help children.

"One day, when I make a lot of money in sports, I'd like to build a day-care center where mothers who work could leave their babies," he told Linda. "It would also be a youth center for teenagers who are like I was—kids in trouble, kids into drugs. It could also be a retirement home kind of place for older folks."

Bo passed the third goal he had set as a freshman: He was picked first in the National Football League draft that April. The Tampa Bay Buccaneers picked him. The Bucs offered Bo a $7.4 million contract for five years of carrying a football.

NFL commissioner Pete Rozelle hands a football to Bo after Bo was picked number one in the 1986 pro football draft. "Jackson Can Wave Baseball Goodbye," newspaper headline writers proclaimed. Sportswriters were sure that Bo would pick a $3 million pro football offer instead of a big league baseball offer of less than a half million dollars. Photo courtesy of Wide World.

One spring day, as Bo roamed centerfield for the Auburn Tigers, a Kansas City Royals baseball scout sat in the stands. He had just heard Coach Baird tell reporters: "Bo could play outfield in the big leagues right now because he owns as strong an arm as I have ever seen. I don't think he is ready to hit major league pitching yet, but all he needs is some at-bats in the minors. People say it takes about a thousand at-bats in the minor leagues—

69

two or three seasons—before a great prospect is ready to hit big league pitching. I think it would take Bo maybe half that number."

About midway through Auburn's 1986 baseball season, Bo was hitting only .245 and he had slammed only 6 home runs. But he told people that he always got off to a slow start in baseball.

The Tampa Bay Bucs asked Bo to fly to Tampa for a physical. Bo flew on a plane owned by the Bucs. Flying on a pro team's plane broke a rule of the Southeastern Conference. The SEC said Bo could play no more college baseball. A sad Bo had to turn in his baseball uniform.

A group of Kansas City Royals officials sat around a table, discussing whom they should pick in the 1986 draft. The talk turned to Bo.

Should they pick Bo? Few teams would pick him—no baseball team could offer him $7 million. Why should a baseball team waste a pick if Bo would certainly choose football?

"He hit only .246 this spring," said one man. "And that's college baseball. People hit .500 all the time in college baseball."

"So why should we pick Bo?"

"Because look at what the scouts say about him."

An official riffled through a sheet of papers. "Dick Egan of the big league scouting bureau says that on a scale of 2 to 8, he rates Bo an 8 for home-run power, an 8 for his throwing arm, and an 8 for speed. Egan says his fielding is weak but fielding is the easiest thing to teach. As for the physical things—speed and strength—Egan says you could scout for a year and never see a guy like Bo."

The Royals picked Bo on the fourth round. He was the 104th player chosen. Each baseball team was sure he would take football's $7.4 million. Within days Bo's phone rang with calls from the Royals and the Bucs. Which team would he choose?

Bo had two business advisers, Richard Woods and

Tom Zieman. They talked to both teams. The Buccaneers offered $3 million plus $4.4 million in bonuses. He would get the bonus money if he gained so many yards in a season, for example, or if he won a season's Most Valuable Player Award. That $7.4 million would be the most ever offered an NFL rookie.

Baseball's Royals wrote a much more modest offer: Bo would be paid $200,000 for 1986. He would get $333,000 if he played in 1987. He would get $383,000 for 1988. Plus he would get a bonus of $150,000 if he was still playing baseball at the end of 1988.

"Football is guaranteeing him three million dollars," Royals co-owner Ewing Kauffman said. "We're guaranteeing him two hundred thousand dollars."

"He'll go for the football money," one of his aides said.

"I hope not. Every scout tells me that Bo could be another Mickey Mantle or Willie Mays."

Bo woke up one morning at Auburn. Baseball or football? Which would it be? He had the answer—baseball!

Then he frowned. If Bo chose baseball, the Royals would send him to the minor leagues. He'd ride for hours in hot, cramped buses. Bo groaned.

Yeah, he'd pick football! But again, he frowned. Football meant practice, practice, practice. He hated practice. And in pro football you were hit by 280-pound express trains. Bo knew one slashing tackle could wreck his knees—what he called "my bread and butter." Those knees had never been operated on by a surgeon. "And," as Bo told friends, "I don't intend they ever will be."

But on the other hand . . . football offered him millions. By comparison, baseball offered him peanuts.

He walked to a class. A friend asked if he had made up his mind. Bo smiled ruefully and said, "I may chuck 'em both and do what I like to do best—go fishing."

Late in May, Bo decided what he would do. He bought an airline ticket to Anaheim, California. His idol, Reggie

71

Jackson, played at Anaheim for the California Angels. Bo and Reggie had met at a sports dinner. Reggie had offered to give Bo advice if he wanted it.

Bo shook hands with Reggie, who looked with some amazement at Bo's muscled body. "I understand," Reggie said, "that scouts think you can hit .300, get 50 homers in a season, and have 50 to 75 stolen bases. That means you can be the best baseball player there ever has been."

Bo said nothing. But he glowed inside. His idol, Reggie Jackson, was saying these things about the kid who had watched Reggie hit those five World Series home runs back in 1977.

For an hour Bo sat entranced as Reggie talked about baseball and what it offered. A baseball career could be longer, Reggie said. Reggie had played in the big leagues for almost twenty years. A football career could be snapped suddenly. Sure, football paid more up front. But if you stuck in baseball, a baseball career could pay more money because you could last longer.

Bo thanked Reggie. He went to the airport and flew back to Auburn. He had made up his mind.

CHICK

"How could you turn down three million dollars a year for two hundred thousand a year?"

Bo smiled at the question thrown at him by a reporter. Bo stood in front of a pack of reporters and a row of TV cameras set up in the office of the Kansas City Royals. It was a warm morning in June, and the Royals had just announced that Bo had signed a contract to play baseball.

"In life you take chances," Bo replied. "My first love was baseball rather than football. My goal is to be the best baseball player Bo Jackson can be. My strengths are my speed and my arm. I need to work on hitting the curveball."

A little later he pulled on a Royals uniform. He wore number 16, not the 34 he'd worn in football at Auburn nor the 29 he had worn there in baseball. He was putting Auburn behind him.

After talking to the reporters, Bo walked out to the batting cage at Royals Stadium. He swung at fastballs thrown by a coach. He drove more than a dozen balls out of the park. "He's built like a football player," said Royals outfielder Willie Wilson. "But he sure hits like a baseball player."

His decision made, Bo dons the baseball cap of the Kansas City Royals. The Royals had picked him on the fourth round of the 1986 draft; other teams ignored Bo, who had been picked on the first round by the Yankees when he was a high school senior. Few baseball teams thought he would choose baseball. As a result, they didn't want to waste a draft pick by choosing him.
Photo courtesy of Wide World.

Bo worked out with the Royals for ten days while the team decided which minor league team he should play for. They sent him to the Memphis Chicks in the Southern Association. The Royals told Bo, "If you do well, we will bring you up to Kansas City in September when the minor league season is over."

A crowd of more than seven thousand filled little Tim McCarver Stadium in Memphis to watch Bo's baseball debut. TV networks sent camera crews to film the event. More than a hundred newspaper writers from across the country sat in the press box. "Never," wrote a *Sporting News* reporter, "had a minor league debut been such a media event."

After announcing he had chosen baseball, Bo is hugged by his mother. She had never liked Bo playing football, fearing he would be injured. A Kansas City scout said of Bo: "I get the feeling I am watching something that comes along once every fifty years or so. Bo is the best pure athlete in America." Photo courtesy of Wide World.

Memphis played the Columbus, Georgia, Astros that night. Memphis Chicks' manager Tommy Jones penciled Bo's name into the seventh-place position in the batting order. Bo would be the Chicks' designated hitter. Jones wanted Bo to polish his fielding before putting him out into centerfield.

Bo came to bat in the first inning. A Chicks runner stood at second base. "Go, Bo, Go!" the crowd chanted.

The Astro pitcher threw a strike. Then he missed with his next two pitches for a count of two and one. Bo flicked the canary yellow bat back and forth, eyeing the pitcher.

A fastball buzzed toward Bo. He swung, and the *craccck!* was loud in the humid night air. The ball bounded

75

up the middle and into centerfield. In his first at-bat as a pro, Bo had collected his first hit for pay.

Bo struck out twice that night. After the game Bo told reporters: "Some people see Bo Jackson as the type of guy who can't be beat, and that's not true. I'm human, just like everybody else. Don't expect too much of Bo because of the name. I have to come into my own . . ."

Bo quickly showed just how human he was. He didn't get a hit in his next game, nor in his next. In his first 27 at-bats, he had only 2 hits, the second a windblown flyball that dropped for a double. His average was a sickly .074.

Back in Kansas City, Royals officials looked at that average. Then they rechecked Bo's Auburn record. In his three seasons at Auburn he had hit .279, .401, and .246. He had played in fewer than 90 games over those three seasons. "You know," said one official, "the one thing that we may have overlooked is that he hasn't played baseball a lot."

Had the Royals made a big mistake in thinking Bo could be a big leaguer?

Southern Association pitchers thought so. "He can't hit Uncle Charlie," one sneered after fanning Bo. "Uncle Charlie" is baseball lingo for the curveball.

Bo struck out 12 times in his first 27 at-bats. Bo said he wasn't worried. "I would rather start off with a slump than start off good and get in a slump," he told other Chicks. "I'd rather start off at the bottom and work up. Life is full of slumps . . . but you can come off them."

Bo came to the ballpark at noon for night games. Sweat streamed down his face as he swung at hundreds of batting-practice pitches. Coaches showed him how to hit the curveball as it "fell off the table," as hitters say.

"When the ball breaks away from you," a coach told the right-handed-hitting Bo, "don't try to pull the ball to leftfield. You will hit the ball straight back to the pitcher or to the second baseman. You have got to go with the pitch as it breaks away from you. You move toward the pitch and slap it to rightfield for a single or a double."

Bo joined the Royals late in the 1986 season. He told people that Reggie Jackson had been the one who had bent him toward baseball. "I probably wouldn't be standing here today if it weren't for Reggie. But now it's time to stop idolizing Reggie and make my own footsteps." Photo courtesy of the Kansas City Royals.

Bo began to whack those curves to rightfield. Speeding around the bases, he sometimes flew around second and slid into third for a triple.

Pitchers began to fire fastballs inside to Bo. Often he swung and missed those inside pitches. His thick shoulders seemed to slow up his bat. But if a pitcher missed inside—the ball zooming across the plate—Bo swept his bat into the pitch. He hit two towering homers that had pitchers shaking their heads. "Can't make a mistake against him," one pitcher said. Bo hit one homer that soared 550 feet, the longest ever hit in the Southern Association.

Bo hit above .350 during July and August. He lifted his batting average to .277. He blasted 7 home runs. He smacked in 25 runs, almost one every two games.

In September, the minor league season ended. The Royals invited Bo to join the big league team for the final three weeks of the American League season. In one of his first games as a Royal, Bo hit a 475-foot homer. Kansas City writers called the homer the longest every hit in Royals Stadium.

Bo finished the season with two homers and a .207 average. The Royals finished third in the American League West, out of the playoffs. Bo flew back to Auburn, Linda, and baseballs.

He went to classes to get his degree. Bo and Linda had married and lived in an apartment near the campus. In the afternoons Bo ran with the Auburn sprinters, showing them tricks he had learned in getting out of the blocks fast. The Royals sent coach Eddie Napoleon to Auburn to improve Bo's pursuit and snaring of low line drives and ground balls. "He had spent so little time playing baseball," Napoleon said later, "he didn't even know how to hold his glove to field ground balls. But he worked and he listened. Because he's such a great athlete, he learned fast."

Bo took batting practice with the Auburn baseball team. He begged pitchers to throw their wickedest curves, their fiercest fastballs. He had only a few months to be ready for spring training.

"In the past I never worked hard because things came fairly easy for me in sports," Bo said. "I haven't worked this hard since my freshman football year at Auburn. But I know that if I hope to be with the Royals this season, I have to work my tail off."

Coach Baird knew how Bo hated to practice. "I am astounded," the coach said. "Bo has completely committed himself to baseball greatness."

That greatness seemed to come fast in the spring of 1987.

RAIDER

"Where is Bo?"

Reggie Jackson stood outside the Royals' dugout at Anaheim Stadium and yelled at the Royals players once more: "Where's Bo?"

"He's in the clubhouse," a Royals coach shouted back.

"Tell him to get out here!"

A few minutes later, Bo and his mentor chatted outside the Royals dugout. Reggie stared at Bo and said with mock anger on his face: "I've played twenty-six hundred games. I hit more than five hundred home runs. But I turn on the TV and all I see is you. You're a superstar already."

Bo laughed. But Reggie was right: It seemed Bo had become an instant superstar. At the beginning of this 1987 baseball season, a writer for *Sports Illustrated* declared: "Everyone's bubbling about Bo." Said Tiger manager Sparky Anderson, "Soon he'll pack stadiums coast to coast."

Royal's outfielder Willie Wilson said he had never seen the likes of Bo. "He can hit a roller to third base and beat it out. Then he can come up the next time and hit one five hundred feet."

Bo had come to the Royals' spring training camp in Florida with less baseball playing time than any player in camp. There had been only those 89 games in college, 53 with the Chicks in the minors, and 25 with the Royals late in 1986.

"Bo's in the process of getting an education that's just started," veteran Royal Hal McRae said. "He may have more talent than anyone in the game, but tools don't count. What counts is your number of hits. Bo's education is going to take three to five years. And those years will include some hard times."

Bo batted .273 in spring training games. He hit 3 home runs. He led all the Royals with 11 runs batted in. In one game he ran a long way to grab a line drive. Then he spun and threw a white rocket to try to nail a runner going from second to third.

Third baseman George Brett slapped the ball on the sliding runner. George yelled to a teammate, "Who says Bo doesn't belong?"

"By the time we broke camp and headed to Kansas City," catcher Jamie Quirk said later, "everyone knew Bo belonged in the big leagues." On opening day of the 1987 season, Bo, a year out of college ball, trotted out of the dugout as the Royals' staring leftfielder.

Early in the season Bo came to bat against Detroit's Dan Petrie. In spring training Petrie had struck out Bo three times in one game. Bo had flailed his bat at veering sliders and curves.

Bo had learned that by raising his left foot as a pitch streaked toward him he delayed swinging the bat. That gave him time to see which way the curve or slider broke. "He can swing a bat so fast," said Hal McRae, "that he can wait until the last second to swing and still pull to left-field."

Bo waited for Petrie to throw a slider. He saw it break and swung. The ball streaked into centerfield for a single.

Bo came up again—and again Petrie broke a slider. Bo cracked that pitch into the leftfield seats.

He came up a third time. Petrie challenged him with a breaking pitch—a curve. Bo, again timing the break, walloped that pitch into the stands for a second home run. Later he hit a 420-foot home run, his third of the game.

The Royals came to New York for a series with the Yankees. Bo led the league with a .492 batting average. Hordes of reporters ringed him as he dressed in the visitors' clubhouse. They asked if the Heisman winner would ever go back to football.

"Bo doesn't talk about that other sport," Bo said, smiling. By now, sportswriters had grown accustomed to Bo calling himself Bo. They knew that he stuttered when he said "I."

The reporters also knew that the Royals feared Bo might quit baseball for football if he slumped as a hitter. The Royals had planned to pay Bo about $1,200,000 from 1986 to 1988. But Bo would have to give back the Royals nearly all of that, about a million dollars, if he decided to play football by July 15 of this 1987 season.

Bo insisted he would never have to return that million dollars. "I don't have time for both sports in a single year," he said. How could he play baseball through October, then go to a football team? The football team would be halfway through the NFL season by October.

"Bo wishes he could have played both baseball and football," Bo said. Then he added, with some doubt in his voice, "But I am told by people that it's not possible." Bo seemed to be wondering if those people were right.

Against the Yankees, Bo struck out five times in one game. He became only the 25th player in the entire history of big league baseball to fan five times in one game.

Bo was striking out at a record rate—about once every three times at bat. If he kept whiffing at this rate, he would break the big league record for striking out—once every 2.92 times at bat.

"Bo always keeps in mind that this strikeout business will end one day," Bo told teammates. "Bo'll be on a tear then. I'm just having a hard time laying off that one pitch— the high fastball. I think once I lay off that"—the high pitch that would be called a ball instead of a strike—"I'll be okay. Then they'll have to give me good pitches, strikes, to swing at."

But his batting average plummeted—from nearly .500 to .260. Royals' manager Billy Gardner benched him when the Royals faced hard-throwing righthanders. Hal McRae took Bo aside and told him not to feel bad. "You get good numbers and you get bad numbers," the veteran said. "That's baseball. Baseball's not a week-to-week thing. To be a star takes three to five years."

Coming home one night after a baseball game, Bo got a message to call an official with the New England Patriots football team. The 1987 NFL draft would begin in a few days. Bo called the Patriots, who asked him: Would he play football if they drafted him?

Bo told the Patriots what he told everyone else. He had promised to play the full baseball season with the Royals. He would keep that promise. If the Royals went to the World Series, he would be playing baseball in October. If he then joined a football team, he would have missed the entire first half of the NFL season. Who wants a player for half a season?

Bo knew that no athlete—not Jim Thorpe sixty years ago, not John Elway in the 1980s—had been able to successfully play both pro football and big league baseball.

But the idea tantalized Bo. He could become the first athlete to play in both a World Series and a Super Bowl— *in the same season!*

"People say I can't be a star in both sports," Bo told friends. "I love to prove people wrong. But I don't know how I can do it."

The Los Angeles Raiders raised eyebrows at the NFL draft. They picked Bo on the twelfth round. The next day reporters crowded around Bo in the Royals' dressing room. Would he sign with the Raiders to play pro football?

Bo sighed. He had heard that question so often he was sick of it. Patiently, he explained that it was impossible to play a full season of baseball and a full season of football.

For the next three days, however, Bo kept hearing the same question: Would he play pro football? Finally, Bo put a sign above his dressing stall. It read: "Don't be stupid and ask any football questions."

On a day late that June, the phone rang in the office of the Kansas City Royals' co-owner Avron Fogelman. Calling was Richard Woods, Bo's agent.

The two men talked briefly. Then Woods gave Fogelman the news that shook the Royals team like an earthquake: *Bo wanted to play pro football this year!*

ROYAL-RAIDER

"Bo will be a baseball player from the first day of spring training each year until the last game we play. Then if he wants, he can play pro football."

The Royals players, seated in their clubhouse, glared at the speaker. He was John Schuerholz, the Royals' general manager. The GM had come to the clubhouse to explain why the Royals had rewritten Bo's contract to allow him to play pro football in the fall of 1987 with the Los Angeles Raiders.

"My contract says I can't even water ski in the winter," the Royals' best hitter, George Brett, said. "How can you let Bo play pro football where one tackle could cripple his knees?"

"I can't even play touch football in the winter," another player growled.

Schuerholz explained Bo's new contract. If Bo got hurt in football and could no longer play baseball, Bo had to give back to the Royals half what they had paid him so far, which was about $200,000.

Would the other Royals be willing to pay back the team if they got hurt playing another sport? The players were silent.

Avron Fogelman talked about that surprise phone call from Bo's agent. "We just didn't want to throw up our hands and say, 'No you can't play football.' That might have soured him on baseball. He could have quit baseball. The Royals and baseball would have lost a rare talent, maybe its greatest player ever. And by letting Bo play both sports, we may be letting him find out that he doesn't really want to play football. I think he'll come back full time to baseball."

But John Schuerholz worried. "The question is, Can a human body hold up being battered in football, then have the strength and agility to play 162 games of baseball? I just don't know."

What made Bo's impossible dream—to play both baseball and football—suddenly possible?

Two weeks earlier Bo's agent, Richard Woods, read a newspaper article about Al Davis, the owner of the Raiders. Davis told a reporter that Bo could play for the Raiders for half a season. "He'd join us in late October," Davis said

Bo and Linda leave a press conference in mid-July of 1987 where Bo announced that he would play the last half of the 1987 NFL season for the Los Angeles Raiders. Both look worried, realizing that players and fans in Kansas City will be angry.
Photo courtesy of Wide World.

in the article. "He could help us win the last eight games of the season and get us into the playoffs and the Super Bowl."

Woods talked to Bo about what Davis had said. Bo's eyes lit up. Maybe this was the way he could play both sports—baseball for an entire season, then football for half a season.

"See what you can do," Bo said to Woods.

The agent talked to Davis. Within ten days they had drawn up a contract that would pay Bo about two and a half million dollars over five seasons. Bo would start working for the Raiders after each baseball season ended.

Royals players looked angrily at Bo when they heard the news. Bo had become one of the team's best run producers. True, he still struck out a lot. But he had kept his average around .250. And he had slugged more home runs than any Royal—18. Now, they thought, Bo had deserted the Royals to be a Raider.

"My number one job is playing for the Kansas City Royals," Bo told them. "I have to do my job with the Royals before I do anything else. Whatever comes after baseball is a hobby for Bo . . ."

A hobby? Did Bo think that the bruising business of pro football was a hobby like stamp collecting? Football and baseball players hooted. "How can being belted by someone like 260-pound Lawrence Taylor be a hobby?" asked Royals outfielder Willie Wilson.

"It is a hobby," Bo said. "I wish I could make money at my favorite hobby—fishing."

When Bo strode to the plate to bat at Royals Stadium, the fans booed. Signs proclaimed their anger: "You turned your back on us!" Fans hurled rubber footballs at Bo.

"I wish that booing would stop," George Brett said. "If they keep booing him, I wouldn't blame him for leaving."

Many football officials said they understood why Bo had signed with the Raiders. "For Bo Jackson," said Dallas Cowboy's vice president Gil Brandt, "one of the greatest thrills in life is to prove others wrong when they say he can't do something."

Bo agreed. "I'm always going to do the opposite of what the public thinks," he said with a grin. "When ninety-nine percent say Bo can't do something, I use that as fuel for my fire. I try to go out and prove them wrong—every time."

Bo tried to calm the stormy waves in Kansas City. "Baseball is my number one priority," he insisted. "Every day I go out onto a field, I learn something. The more I play, the better I will get."

The Royals players still were angry. One posted a sign over Bo's stall that read: "Don't be stupid and ask any baseball questions." When Bo saw the sign, he ripped it down.

Bo's best friend on the team, rightfielder Danny Tartabull, looked concerned. "Everybody is upset," Danny said. "I hope all this doesn't distract the other players and destroy the team."

The boos seemed to draw Bo's eyes away from baseballs. He struck out more often. His average sunk even lower. In 25 at-bats after announcing he would play football, Bo rapped out only 4 hits. In 16 of those 25 at-bats, he struck out. Perhaps worse, he stopped hitting home runs.

"Bo is letting the game and the booing get to him," said George Brett, a veteran who had seen other young players shaken by a crowd's loud booing. "You can't let the strikeouts and the failures get you down. Each day has got to be a new day. But I see Bo coming to the ballpark looking like he dreads facing another bad day."

Flyballs began to zip by Bo's glove in leftfield. "Catching a flyball," one writer said, "is becoming an adventure for Bo."

The Royals still snapped at the heels of the Minnesota Twins in the race for first in the American League West. In July, Billy Gardner began to put in pinch hitters for Bo when Bo came to bat with runners on second or third.

Bo sat on the bench, silent. But later he told Linda, "There are days when I don't want to go to the ballpark. And there are days when I just want to leave."

By August Bo sat on the bench nearly all the time, no longer a starter and only occasionally a designated hitter or pinch hitter. "They don't want me in there during the pennant race," Bo angrily told Linda.

Late in September the Twins forged ahead of the Royals to win the AL West (and, later, the 1987 World Series). The Royals fired Billy Gardner. The new manager, John Wathan, put Bo into the starting lineup.

"I guess I could say I don't want to play now that the games mean nothing," Bo said. "But that's not my style."

Fans booed Bo. They blamed him because the Royals had finished two games behind the Twins. When George Brett heard the boos, he threw up his hands and said, "How could Bo lose the race for us when he played so little?"

Bo finished the season with respectable statistics for a rookie. He had batted only .235 but he had hit 22 home runs, more than any other Royal except Brett and Willie Wilson.

Trouble was, crowed the critics, Bo hit only .188 in the last half of the season. And he hit only 2 of those 22 home runs in the last half of the season.

How could he hit home runs or lift his batting average, said Bo, when he was sitting on the bench or coming into games feeling rusty after not playing for a week?

Bo had a point, said the critics. But after he agreed to play football, they said, he just didn't seem to be as fearsome at the plate as he had been in the first half of the season. And at times, they said, he seemed to be thinking of other things as he chased line drives in leftfield.

"Bo just wasn't the same player in the second half that he was in the first half," said John Schuerholz. "But Bo can still be one of the all-time greats, especially if he concentrates on baseball."

Other experts agreed. They pointed to Bo's strikeout

total—158 times in 396 at-bats—and reminded fans that most great sluggers strike out a lot. Babe Ruth did. And Mickey Mantle struck out more often than anyone in baseball history.

When Bo didn't strike out—when his bat met the ball—the ball often flew for base hits. Baseball writer Murray Chass figured out that when Bo hit the ball, he had a batting average of .391.

By now the Jacksons were three—Linda had given birth to a baby boy who was christened Garrett. Bo nicknamed him Spud. Linda, Bo, and Spud went back to their apartment in Auburn. Linda was studying for a doctorate in child psychology.

The 1987 NFL season had come to a stop after its first two weeks. The players went on strike, asking for better contracts. After three weeks the strike ended and Bo flew to Los Angeles to report to the Raiders.

Bo wore his old Auburn football number, 34. During his first workout, he grabbed a pitchout from the quarterback and sprinted for the sideline. A big tackle caught him from behind and wrestled him to the turf.

Raiders' coach Tom Flores watched from the sideline, a frown on his bony face. "Bo may be in shape for baseball," Flores said. "But he's not in shape for football."

AWESOME

Bo sat down on the stool in the clubhouse. Facing him on another stool sat Marcus Allen. A spindly-legged, broad-shouldered running back, Marcus was the Raiders' number one ground-gainer. Raiders players thought that Marcus, a Heisman winner, might be jealous when Bo arrived. But Marcus and Bo soon were pals. "We need a second running back," Marcus told people. "Other teams gang up to stop me. Now, if they do, we can spring Bo loose."

"I've lost a step of speed running to the outside," Bo told Marcus. "I'm getting older. And I've gained weight. I'm 230. I was only 222 in college. The extra years and the extra pounds, they cost me a step."

"Stop thinking about it. Just use that extra weight as power to run over guys."

Other Raiders thought Bo as quick as a pesky fly. "When I hand the ball to Bo," quarterback Marc Wilson said, "he's gone by me and I'm still holding the ball in my hands."

But Bo felt he was sticky and slow compared to his last year at Auburn. The Raiders met the New England Patriots on November 1. Bo watched most of the game on the sideline, replacing Marcus Allen whenever Marcus needed a breather. Bo ran the ball 8 times and gained 37 yards but the Raiders lost, 26–23.

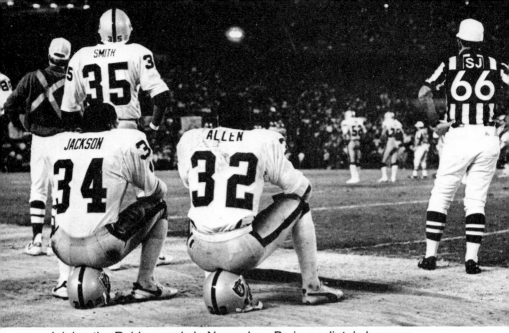

Joining the Raiders early in November, Bo immediately became friendly with Marcus Allen, another Heisman winner and the team's number one running back. Talking to reporters, Bo said, "I came here to contribute what I have to the Royals." It was a slip of the tongue; he meant, of course, the Raiders.
Photo courtesy of the Los Angeles Raiders.

Bo ran hard all week, trying to regain that lost step. The following Sunday, against the Vikings, he ran 12 times and gained 74 yards. Bo could not break away for one of his long scoring streaks. The Raiders lost, 31–20.

The Super Bowl champions in 1981, the Raiders drove toward touchdowns like a wobbly arrow, usually falling short of the mark. "We need someone—a passer, a runner—to put hard steel into our attack," Coach Flores told reporters.

During practice the following week, Bo suddenly seemed to find wings for his feet. Now he had that extra burst of takeoff speed that had shot him away from tacklers as the Heisman winner a year earlier. When he burst up the middle, tacklers seemed to bounce off him. "He could be the best running back in the NFL," defensive back Carl Lee said. "He's big and fast, but a lot of guys are big and fast. What makes Bo different is that he can keep his balance even when 250-pound linebackers are slamming into him. He won't go down."

The Raiders lost their sixth straight game, beaten by Green Bay, 16–14. Bo ran the ball 8 times and gained 48 yards. He led the team with an average of better than 5 yards a run, topping Marcus' average of 4.

The Raiders next faced the Denver Broncos, a team streaking toward its second straight Super Bowl. The Broncos burst out to a 13–0 lead. The Raiders tried to rally. Bo and Marcus drove inside and outside and brought the ball to the Denver 35.

In the huddle Marc Wilson called for a sweep to the right, Bo carrying the ball. Bo sprinted toward the right sideline behind a wave of blockers. Broncos stripped the blockers away. Bo saw two Denver tacklers crouched, waiting for him, arms stretched wide.

Bo stopped, spun, and sped the opposite way—to the left sideline. His flyaway speed propelled him ahead of a pack of pursuers. First to reach the sideline, Bo curled downfield, the pack puffing behind him. Only one Bronco stood between Bo and the goal—blocky cornerback Mike Hardin.

Bo had been zigzagging away from tacklers all day. Now he remembered Marcus's advice—run over them!

Bo bent his head and rammed full steam into Hardin. The Bronco bounced backward like a flattened bowling pin. Stretched on his back, he stared upward as Bo soared over him. "That," Hardin said later, a look of amazement on his face, "never happened to me before."

Bo scooted down the sideline to the 5. Three Broncos cornered him. Bo dived over them like an Olympic gymnast, somersaulting into the end zone for his first NFL touchdown.

A video replay of that spectacular run was looked at on TV screens by millions during the week. NFL players and coaches gasped when they saw Bo's power in running over Hardin and his agility in diving over the three tacklers. "That," said Seattle coach Chuck Knox, "was a Hall of Fame play."

Bo ran for a second touchdown against the Broncos, but Denver won, 23–17. The Raiders had dropped their seventh straight. Their record was now a sickly 3–7.

Bo averaged better than 6 yards a run, tops in the NFL. As the Raiders prepared to play Chuck Knox's Seattle Seahawks, Coach Flores came to a decision.

He asked Marcus Allen to come to his office.

Millions of Americans switched on their TV sets. They had been reading about Bo Jackson. They had watched him play big league baseball during the summer. Now, on this Monday night football game in late November, they wanted to see him trying to play pro football. This was Bo's first pro football game on national TV. "He's scored a couple of touchdowns," fans were saying, "but he's played only part time."

Now Bo would play full time. Coach Flores had made him the team's number one ball carrier, putting him in Marcus' tailback position. Bo would carry the ball most of the time. Marcus Allen had shifted to blocking back. "I don't mind," Marcus said, "because I'm a team player and we have got to do something to start winning."

As Bo pulled on his shoulder pads in a dressing room at Seattle's Kingdome, a Raider teammate slapped him on the back. "Happy birthday, Bo!" the player shouted.

Bo grinned. This was Monday night, November 30, 1987—Bo's 25th birthday. He would make it a memorable one.

More than sixty-two thousand people filled the Kingdome. They roared as the Seahawks bounced Bo back for no gain. They roared louder when Bo rushed into the scrimmage line and two Seahawks dropped him in his tracks.

"Yes, Bo's scored a couple of touchdowns," more than one fan said, watching his TV set. "But he just can't jump from one sport to another and expect to be outstanding."

Running against the Denver Broncos, Bo twists away from tacklers.
His sudden success surprised even Bo. "I didn't think my impact

would be as big as it's been. I just came here to contribute. I didn't expect this." Photo courtesy of Wide World.

Seattle scored to lead, 7–0. Marc Wilson whipped a long pass to wide receiver Jim Lofton to tie the game 7–7.

The Raiders pounded to the Seattle 14. Wilson stepped back into the pocket and looked downfield. He saw Bo twist away from a defender near the goal line.

Wilson whistled a pass that Bo grabbed in the end zone. The Raiders led, 14–7.

A little later Bo took a handoff and shot straight up the middle—past the 50 . . . past the 40 . . . past the 30. Two Seahawks knocked him down at the Seattle 23—a 42-yard jaunt that put the Raiders within striking distance of another score.

The Raiders crunched to the 2-yard line. Wilson gave the ball to Bo, who ran wide toward the right sideline. There crouched six-feet-seven, 275-pound linebacker Brian "Boz" Bosworth, looking as hard as a brick wall.

Bo ran straight into Bosworth. Boz toppled backward as though someone had chopped off his knees. Bo danced into the end zone for his second touchdown.

"Bo," a Raider said, "went through Bosworth like Boz was Swiss cheese."

A few minutes later the Raiders held the ball at their 9-yard line. Backed up almost into their end zone, the Raiders decided on a safe sweep to the left side by Bo. Wilson took the snap from center and flipped the ball to Bo. He caught the ball in full stride as though streaking for the finish line in the Olympics.

Bo left Seahawks trailing behind him. At the sideline he sped downfield with safety Kenny Easley, one of the NFL's fastest players, at his heels. Bo pulled away from Easley, a Raider said later, "like Kenny was running in syrup."

That 91-yard touchdown run was the longest ever unreeled by a Raider. It was the eighth longest run from scrimmage in NFL history.

"It happened so fast that I couldn't believe he'd run ninety-one yards," said one NFL coach who watched the game on TV. "I had turned around to grab a sandwich and

After the game Bo shakes hands with Brian Bosworth, the Seattle giant whom he bowled over for a touchdown. A few days later a minor league basketball team asked Bo to play for them. "I don't know how to play basketball," Bo said. "I never did." Another Raider suggested, kidding, that Bo try out for the 1988 U.S. Olympic ski team. Photo courtesy of the Los Angeles Raiders.

when I turned back, he was in the end zone. I thought he'd run for nine yards—not ninety-one."

Bo ran for 221 yards during the Raiders' 37–14 rout. That was the most yardage ever gained in one game by a Raider running back and was the 19th best performance by any running back in NFL history. "Just suppose what he would do," one coach said, "if he had the chance to practice this summer like the rest of the running backs."

"For the first time in a long time," said veteran Raider end Howie Long, "I got chills down my spine watching someone else. Everyone I talk to says the same thing—he's the best runner they have ever seen."

Up in ABC-TV's broadcasting booth, Frank Gifford stumbled over words as he talked about Bo. A Hall of Fame running back with the New York Giants, Gifford had seen dazzling displays of running over the past twenty years by other Hall of Famers like Jim Brown and O. J. Simpson.

"Bo Jackson," Gifford said in a voice that seemed in a state of shock, "could be greater than anyone ever. Tonight he was awesome, simply awesome."

In one year Bo had been awesome as a college runner, awesome as a baseball slugger for half a season, and awesome as a pro football running back for a quarter of a season. True, like lightning flashing across the sky, he had shown his brilliance only briefly in big league baseball and football.

But the brilliance had been there in all its electric excitement. Could the lightning flash longer and brighter—and could it go on flashing each summer in baseball, each autumn in football?

Bo had his own opinions—opinions he was happy to share.

JUST BO

"They'll probably throw rubber baseballs at me."

Bo was speaking to a group of reporters in early December of 1987. The Raiders had just returned from Buffalo, where they had walloped the Buffalo Bills, 34–21. Bo had gained 78 yards running, another 59 by catching passes. On the plane ride home, Coach Flores said to a friend, laughing, "Can we start the whole season over again, right now—but this time with Bo?"

"Yes," said pass catcher Dokie Williams, "Bo has made a difference. He lit a fire under us."

The Raiders next would play the Kansas City Chiefs in Kansas City. The game would be played in Arrowhead Stadium, only a long baseball throw from Royals Stadium, where Bo had hit home runs for the Royals that summer— and where angry fans had thrown rubber footballs at him.

Bo led the NFL with an average of 7 yards a run. Reporters were talking to him a few days before the Raiders flew to Kansas City to play the Chiefs. After a month of bruising knocks in the NFL, did Bo still think he could play both baseball and football?

Bo laughed. "You know," he said, "I get a kick out of hearing people say, 'I knew that he could play in the NFL.' Those are the same people who said that I would never make it in the NFL. I get as much fun out of making people liars as I get by going out and playing."

But then he added quickly: "The pounding I take in football will eventually take its toll. When the time comes to give up a sport, I will give one up. And I would say it probably will be football. But right now football is number one in my heart. Ask me next summer what's number one in my heart and I will tell you that baseball is number one in my heart.

"I feel I have the God-given ability to display talents in both sports, and I'm going to do that. But there's going to be a time when I'm going to give up a sport, I know that. The only question is, When will I give up football? Baseball's what I will make a career out of—not football. Right now, I'm just taking this one day at a time."

"You seem to be having a lot of fun playing football," a reporter said.

"You can only be young once," Bo said. "And I am going to have all the fun I can."

Bo, Linda, and Garrett—Spud—lived in a rented apartment high above the Pacific Ocean in nearby Redondo Beach. Bo drove to the house after practice in his sleek sports car. Often the car moved as slowly as an inchworm, hemmed in by other cars. Bo told a friend, "It takes me an hour to go to the supermarket, and it's only a mile away from where we live."

One afternoon, as Bo played with Spud in the living room of the apartment, the building shook. Bo leaped up from the floor. Linda ran into the room. "What's that?" she shrieked.

Bo held the frightened Linda and Spud in his arms and said grimly, "Another earthquake."

Within a month the building shook four times, rattled by earthquakes that erupted across California. "Between the traffic jams and the quakes," Bo told Linda, "I am going to be glad when the season ends and we are back safe and sound in our condo in Kansas City."

One evening Bo and Linda drove to nearby Beverly

Hills, where many TV and movie stars live. Linda wanted to shop for clothes. As Bo and Linda walked up a street, other shoppers stopped to stare at them.

A little girl asked Bo for his autograph. Linda was surprised. "These people here know you," Linda said. She knew Bo was famous in Auburn and Kansas City, but he had been in California only a month and already he was a famous person.

Bo and Linda stopped to eat at a restaurant. "It's funny," Bo told Linda after they had ordered, "how a guy like me can come from a small town back South, come out here where there are thousands of famous people, and have all these people recognize you."

The Raiders flew to Kansas City. A Kansas City TV station asked its viewers whether they would cheer for Bo or boo him. Five of ten said they'd boo, the other five said they'd cheer.

The cheers were mixed with boos as Bo ran out onto the field with the other Raiders. Bo saw one sign hanging from the stands. A fan had painted a jackass on the sign. The word "Bo" had been painted on the head of the jackass.

"I like that sign," Bo said to another player. "We all have a little jackass in us now and then."

Early in the game Bo ran into the line. The Chiefs threw him backward. The crowd of more than sixty-three thousand roared its delight.

Bo got up slowly. His shoe had caught in the grass. He had heard something pop in his right ankle.

But he stayed in the game. The ankle hurt. Bo dropped back to block for Marc Wilson as the quarterback looked downfield for an open receiver. A Kansas City tackle slammed into Bo and bowled him over.

Bo limped off the field. He still remembered how, at Auburn, he had tried to play when hurt and had damaged a shoulder. Bo told Coach Flores he had hurt the ankle and could not run. A trainer looked at the swollen ankle and told Bo it was sprained.

"Whew!" Bo said, relieved. "When I heard that pop, I thought it might have been The Big One." The Big One, to football players, is the injury that ends a career.

Bo had carried the ball only 3 times. All 3 times the Chiefs knocked him backward for a total loss of 1 yard. The Chiefs won, 16–10.

That loss dashed the slim chance that the Raiders would make the playoffs. They had two games to play. The Raiders told Bo to sit out those two games. They didn't want that sprained ankle to become The Big One.

In less that half a season Bo had gained 554 yards; Marcus Allen had gained 754 over the full season. Bo's average gain, 6.8 yards, was almost twice Marcus's average of 3.8.

Bo had been paid $668,000 for that half a season. If he kept on playing for the Raiders through 1991, he would earn more than $3 million for playing each half-season. Reporters asked him, "Do you think you are worth that much money for half a season's work?"

"I'll earn my keep," Bo said.

Early in 1988, the ankle strong again, Bo began to work out with Auburn's baseball team. Bo told friends that he knew he had a lot of work ahead of him before he could call himself a proven big league baseball player. He knew that the Royals had been disappointed by his weak hitting and fielding in the last half of the 1987 season. But he also knew what the Royals new manager, John Wathan, had said: "Bo's just too great a talent for us to say, 'We don't want you anymore,' "

"I'll go to the minor leagues to work to make myself better if the Royals say I should," Bo told his agent, Richard Woods. The Royals had said that Bo would have to beat out a rookie, Gary Thurman, during spring training to win the starting job in leftfield.

Bo came to Florida six days earlier than the other Royals. At nine each morning, the sun beating down on the diamond, Bo stood in a batting cage and swung at pitches.

"When I took batting practice last year," he told a friend, "I swung for the fences. Now I just swing to meet the ball. I want to hit line drives, not home runs."

"You can't get a base hit," a coach told him, "if you don't contact the ball with the bat."

"Yes, sir," said a Royal who overheard. "When you don't make contact, that's one strike closer to another K." "K" is baseball shorthand for a strikeout.

After batting practice, Bo raced to the outfield. Sweat streamed down his face as he chased after hundreds of line drives hit by coaches to his right and left.

Watching one day was general manager John Schuerholz, who said to a reporter, "Bo's doing everything expected of him—and more."

On opening day at Royals Stadium, Bo trotted out to

The relaxed Bo tells people that nothing will change him as a person. When he goes back to see friends at Auburn, he is saying, he will be wearing a pair of jeans and a sweatshirt. As always, he says, "I'll just be Bo." Photo courtesy of the Los Angeles Raiders.

leftfield. Gary Thurman sat on the bench. Royals fans had read how hard Bo had worked in spring training. When he came up to bat, the fans roared their applause. Even when Bo struck out, Bo heard only a few boos.

But he was striking out a lot. In his first 100 at-bats in the 1988 season, he struck out 33 times, more than anyone in the big leagues. His batting average hung at a miserable .115.

Bo came early to the park for extra batting practice. But he told himself not to worry. "I've learned," he said, "that the more you try harder in this game, the more you press, and then the more you mess up."

Line drives began to stream off his bat. Some of those liners soared high over fences for mammoth home runs. By June Bo's batting average had leaped to almost .300. He led all the Royals with eight homers. And when he hit a line drive for a single, he often turned the single into a "double" by stealing second base. He led all the Royals with 10 stolen bases.

Royals fans thundered applause for Bo as he snapped throws from leftfield to nail runners trying to stretch singles into doubles. His six assists led all Royal outfielders. And in game after game he soared high to pull down line drives that seemed sure homers or he skidded across the turf on his chin to make shoestring catches that turned base hits into outs.

Pitchers growled that Bo no longer whiffed so often. By mid-season, in fact, two All-Star sluggers, the Yanks' Jack Clark and the Reds' Eric Davis, were striking out more often than Bo.

"Bo can hit home runs to beat you," said Milwaukee's Paul Molitor, "and he can steal bases to beat you. He can beat you with his arm or with his glove. He can do so many things to beat you that it's frightening."

His Royal teammates had come to realize that Bo could be a star for both seasons—football and baseball. "We blamed him for all our problems last season when we lost the pennant," said centerfielder Willie Wilson. "At a time when he needed us the most, we abandoned him. He didn't need that abuse, especially from his teammates."

As the 1988 baseball season came to an end, fans and players agreed: Bo Jackson was more than a football player trying to be a big league baseball player. Bo Jackson was a big league baseball player who had climbed to Superman heights, a player who might become a first in American sport history—a superstar in two big-league sports. *The Sporting News,* in fact, asked in a headline, "Has Jackson Become the World's Best Athlete?"

Said George Brett to a friend: "Bo Jackson can do anything in sports that he wants to do."

One day a reporter told Bo, "I predict that you will be the first guy to play in both a World Series and a Super Bowl."

"That would be something very special," Bo said. "But right now I have what I always wanted. I am one of the guys on this baseball team. I couldn't be happier than I am right now."

The twin tracks of careers in pro football and big league baseball stretched ahead for Vincent Bo Jackson. Those tracks could carry him to the Super Bowl or to the World Series—or to both. Bo knew that time would change Vincent Bo Jackson as time had changed Boar Jackson into Bo Jackson. But he told friends that the essential Bo Jackson would not change.

"Sure, it'll be nice having things you never had before," he said, speaking of the millions of dollars that baseball and football were pouring on him. "But it's not going to change me as a person. Years from now, when I come back to visit Auburn for a football game or whatever, I won't be in a big limousine and I won't be wearing a three-piece suit. I'll be in a pair of jeans and maybe a sweatshirt, just like now. I'll just be Bo."

INDEX

Dallas Cowboys, 86
Denver Broncos, 92
Downtown Athletic Club, 64, 66
Dye, Pat, 19–20, 22, 24, 26–27, 30, 33, 36–37,
    39–40, 54, 58

Elway, John, 49, 82

Flores, Tom, 89, 91, 93, 99
Florida, University of, 39, 59
Florida State University, 39
Fogelman, Avron, 83–84

Gardner, Billy, 82, 87–88
Garrett, Linda. *See* Jackson, Linda
Georgia, University of (Bulldogs), 20, 24–25, 32,
    46–47, 60–61, 62–63
Georgia Tech, 39
Green Bay Packers, 92
Greenwood, Jon, 52–53

Heisman Trophy, 22, 40, 45–46, 54, 58–60, 63–
    65, 67, 81, 90–91

Iron Bowl, 27, 40, 61–63

Jackson, Vincent (Bo)
    big league baseball career of, 78–88, 102–105
    childhood years of, 5–11, 65–66
    college baseball career of, 32–35, 41, 46–49,
        52–53, 67, 69–70, 76, 78
    college football career of, 19–31, 36–41, 43–
        47, 54–68
    college student, 35–37, 49–51, 67–68, 78
    college track career of, 32–33, 42, 47
    minor league baseball career of, 73–78
    pro football career of, 84–86, 89–102
Jackson, Linda, 51, 68, 78, 88–89, 100–101

108